THE QUESTIONER:
THOUGHTS OF A POETIC MAN

Jonathan Pool

Co-author
English With Animals
More English With Animals
English Through Scientists

Author
Lid Off a Daffodil: A book of Palindromes
Venus In A Winter Coat
John Henry's Collection Of Comical Dogs
John Henry's Parade of Pet Poems
Broadstairs: Opal Of The Isle

The Questioner:
Thoughts of a Poetic Man

Jonathan Pool

JANUS PUBLISHING COMPANY
London, England

First published in Great Britain 2012
by Janus Publishing Company Ltd,
93–95 Gloucester Place,
London W1U 6BY

www.januspublishing.co.uk

British Library Cataloguing-in-Publication Data
A catalogue record for this book is available from the British Library

ISBN 978-1-85756-763-2

Cover Design: Baker
www.jackets.moonfruit.com

Printed and bound in Great Britain

Contents

Preface

I would hesitate to call the poems which appear in these pages a sonnet sequence. There is nothing sequential in the thoughts which originated in the mind of the questioner apart from the fact, which will not escape the discerning reader, that they all evolved in sonnet form: some Shakespearean, some Petrarchan and others in a variety of structures which do not fall into traditional categories.

A traditional sonnet sequence was presented as a series of fourteen-line verses adhering to a particular theme – one theme in fact, love or beauty or nature, and such a series appealed to those who found the concentration of poetic insight falling within a relatively narrow field. Given the theme, which soon became apparent upon reading some half a dozen verses, the reader then looked for variation of expression which lauded the exquisite shape of a mistress' eyebrow or the sensuousness of golden, cherry lips of perhaps the lambency of a feminine eye. Such delights emanating from the poet's mind were quite naturally transferred to the diligent reader who felt elevated by the poet's vision and shared in his deeply felt appreciation of youthful grace and feminine beauty.

In disdaining to call *Thoughts of a Poetic Man* a sequence, I do so for the simple reason that the questioner has attempted to render into verse every kind of poetic experience which has beset him during the course of a literary lifetime. These thoughts do not appear in the form of a sequence like a series of digits or a musical scale but rather as a diversity or a series of sequences. They constitute a range of poetic imagery and expression upon as many topics, as many subjects and as many themes and ideas and enquiries as would appear seemly in a work of this kind.

For a poet to fix his fancy on an adorable woman and extol her charms and virtues is a delightful thing. Wisdom has it, quite rightly, that love makes the world go round and that is as it should be. But when the world stops spinning while the poet has his dinner then it is possible that his mind or his fancy may drift and dwell on other things, even if it is merely the quality of the roast beef he is attempting to dispatch. If he, the poet, is something more than a gross sensualist or epicure, it is possible that his thoughts might take him into more distant regions, into spheres where abstracted philosophers are apt to wander while speculating on the nature of existence or the purpose of human life upon the third planet. While savouring his red wine and admiring his beloved as she demolishes the last of the baked potatoes – no matter how beautiful they are or may seem to be they do, of course, have to fortify the inner woman – if the poet happens to be interested in the welfare of mankind he might turn the tumble of his thoughts upon the tribal animosities which so often afflict the human race and at the risk of dyspepsia reflect why one group makes war upon another group whose beliefs happen to differ from its own.

It may be that the poet is as concerned for the cultivation of his mind as other men are in the development of their bodies. What is muscle to one man is gristle to another; what is power to the arm of an athlete is strength to the mind of an academic. If the poet habitually takes pains to improve the quality of his mind and hones the refinement of this sensiblilities, then no doubt when he comes to put pen to paper in order to set down the impulses which drive him to shape his thoughts into some kind of poetic shape, then it is to be hoped that his mental training will manifest itself in his chosen medium of expression.

The fourteen-line verse by its very form is a challenge to a poet to compress his thoughts into one hundred and forty syllables. There is no room for error. There is no space in which mentally to meander. Thoughts, emotions, feelings have to be concentrated within a small compass. There is no latitude for words which do not have power at their base. The thought, the thinking needs to be shaped, fashioned hard and sharp as a diamond, hopefully brilliant cut.

Given that the poet has enjoyed his beef and claret and his fair one has decamped to the powder room, he is at liberty to follow up his train of thought, which one day may plague him with questions concerning the validity of the Big Bang and on another may prompt him to bring to the attention of modern astronomical theorists the work of the ancient Hindu philosophers, q.v. *The Chandogya Upanishad*, Book Six, V1, ii, who speculated long before Christ appeared in Bethlehem that in the beginning the universe was Not-Being and that from Not-Being Being was born. And while he, the postprandial poet, is musing on the Singularity and the essence of Not-Being, he questions the defensive attitude of the theoretical experts who do not permit the question to be asked, 'What happened before The Big Bang?' If it really happened that some 15,000,000,000 years ago there was a very loud noise and the universe and all the matter in it came into existence (this estimate has recently been amended to 13,000,000,000) then perhaps the enlightened ones would care to speculate on the state of play in the year 13,000,000,000 and one?

The question concerns the poet. In his quest for the wherewithal that he may be better equipped to resolve the ideas that teem in his mind – he cannot pour from an empty bucket – he feels that he has the right, as do other men, to ask common-sense questions about every aspect of the human condition. These are brilliant minds which are able to calculate the eons that have passed since life began, but we literary men are still likely to say, 'Come on, tell us more! Was there really a vast amount of space with no matter in it? And did the matter just appear?' That would be a miracle – some miracle! 'Who performed it? God?' A well-nourished mind given to flexing its muscle likes to ask questions. It is as natural in some men to ask questions as it is for the chimpanzee to poke a stick into a hole to see if he can find ants to dine on. 'The sharp edge of a razor is difficult to pass over; thus the wise say the path to Salvation is hard.'

Neither is the questioner concerned merely with scientific, biological and evolutionary matters. His verse is likely to range over every aspect of human experience, as much as can be crammed into a life the parameters of which are widely set. Thus, a goodly number of poems deal with people, interesting, ordinary people, those whose lives have made an impact on folk around them. In their way they have been distinctive and memorable: a headmaster, a marine insurance broker, a company director, a housewife, a beachcomber, a lady swimmer, a hungry Irishman, some labourers, a surgeon, a young woman whose house was twice struck by lightning, a Spanish boy whose ear was burnt by his grandmother, an inventive chef who assisted Florence Nightingale at Scutari, a poor woman whose face had been battered by her brute of a husband, a suicide bomber, the metric martyr, a yachtsman whose life I saved, maladroit Uncle Harry, Audrey attacked by a seagull, the young lad at school who said he had three fathers and so on. There are also poems about Queen Elizabeth II, Prince Albert, Sophie, Countess of Wessex, the President of Iran, Saddam Hussain, Field Marshal Montgomery and Caiaphas, High Priest of The Sanhedrin.

In between the scientific verses and the poems about people, the diligent reader will find a number of references to religion. Millions of people on this planet may be deemed religious as a result of their yearning for a God, a Supreme Being, an Eternal Father, a Creator who engenders life and is worshipped in chapels, churches, cathedrals, mosques, temples and meeting places throughout the world. This is a beautiful thing, as natural as the love and affection which sustains family life. Faith in an omnipotent, omnipresent, all-forgiving, loving God who, like the good shepherd, watches over his flock, succours and comforts his creatures be they Christian, Jewish, followers of Islam, Hindu, Sikh, Zoroastrian or whatever. As a religion is unquestionably a powerful influence in the transient lives of the inhabitants of this planet, it is not surprising that the questioner should find himself penning verses about this supremely important subject; but what is alarming among the religionists who adhere to their various faiths is that they are so imbued with the tenets and dogmas of their beliefs that they become intolerant of those whose creeds and modes of worship are different from their own. This intolerance leads inevitably to a hardening of attitude which so very easily results in conflict, not only verbal conflict but physical violence of the worst kind leading to war, killing, massacre and murder. How can religious people of any faith resort to violence and killing when the god they worship is said to be a god of love? God, Jehovah, Allah, Brahma, Ahura Mazda – what is the difference? A rose by any other name is still a rose – sweet, fragrant, lovely, tender, a symbol of love as all flowers must be. To crush a rose is unforgivable; to kill a human being because of a difference in belief is an appalling crime which cannot be easily forgiven! 'Thou shalt not kill!' saith the Lord, thy God. That commandment is surely common to all faiths?

A glance through the history books at the references to religious intolerance, wars, massacres, inquisitions, heresies, crusades, Catholic plots, Protestant counter plots, burnings, brutalities among Moslems and Hindus during the partition of India – the list is horrifying and the consequences of religious hatreds simply revolting! And now, at the present time, mankind has to endure a new, even more evil horror – the cult of the suicide bomber who, in his deluded state, kills himself and hundreds of innocent people who are sensibly and happily getting on with their lives. God sitting in His heaven must feel revulsion at the atrocities committed by religionists whose mental state leads them to fanaticism. The compassionate reader will perhaps pause and reflect awhile when he turns to the poem which advocates the abolition of religion and understands that it is an exercise in logic: no guns – no shooting; no whips – no lashing; no knives – no stabbing: no criminals – no crime!

What a beautiful world this could be if The Almighty were to stir Himself somewhat and through His intermediaries forbid evils which are being committed in his name!

The interested reader who is concerned about the impact which religion seems to have on so many people whose tolerance cannot take one step beyond what they have been taught to believe, should read the relevant sections, Religion and Intellect, in a book entitled *The Martyrdom of Man*. Written by Winwood Reade and first published in the year 1872, it is a vivid prose epic which asserts the infancy of man's beliefs and advocates their abolition in the most forthright terms in order to force mankind to be more resourceful, mature and responsible in its attitude towards the human condition. A man should develop his intellect and open his mind, Reade writes, and realise that in the words of the poet, William Ernest Henley, 'I am the master of my fate, I am the captain of my soul.'

The questioner is very happy to assure the reader that although he is from time to time inclined to dwell on the infirmities which afflict mankind, he is not without some light in his eye and an enduring sense of humour. In fact, on many occasions in his writing, he finds the instinct for comedy leading him along the byways of humour, in which he has been known to laugh aloud at some comic or amusing incident which has finished up on the written page. The questioner's hope is that what appeals to him may in turn appeal to someone else! If we can help one another spread a little heavenly laughter abroad then surely it may, in the words of Sellar and Yeatman, be accounted 'a good thing!' The writer makes no excuse for presuming to introduce humour into a sonnet. It won't do any harm. It may upset a few purists who like to believe what they have been taught – that the sonnet is essentially a lyric poem written to express individual or private emotions – but it is on record that in the seventeenth century John Donne and John Milton extended the range from love and romance to include religious themes and contemplation upon serious matters.

Therefore the questioner, following precedent, has extended the mode further by introducing less serious matters and, where appropriate, a becoming sense of wit and delight. In fact it cannot be helped – that is the way the questioner is. His smile, his sense of humour, his mental gaiety will out and who is to say it should not be or must not be expressed in this way at this particular time! He insists that the time is most appropriate for a lessening of tension in a complex, dangerous world in which conflict and human misery blacken the front pages of our daily newspapers so often that the perceptive reader longs for the day when a sunburst of humour and bonhomie lights up the columns of death and morbidity!

The questioner sent some poems to the Literary Review a few years ago which were light-hearted and comic. They were not published. In a subsequent issue of the magazine the editor wrote that humour had no place in poetry! Really? Had the dear man never come across the work of Edward Lear, Ogden Nash and A. A. Milne? Milne's couplet from Teddy Bear in *When We Were Very Young*:

'A bear, however hard he tries,
Grows tubby without exercise.'

is absolutely delightful. No doubt the editor meant to assert that humour had no place in poetry *in his magazine*, i.e. that he did not want comic verse to appear in its scholarly pages. So be it. The questioner, on the other hand, does not object to serious and light-hearted material appearing in his pages and in fact, he found it extremely difficult to prevent humorous pieces from insinuating themselves into his collection and insisting on being heard. Exercising the kind of tolerance which he advocates in other spheres, the writer recommends that the reader turns in the following pages to *Humour In A Sonnet*, or *An Immortal Kiss*, or *Drilling Cheek to Cheek*, or even to the poem in three parts, *Mother and Her Eels*. It is the questioner's wish that the reader finds pleasure in the comic as well as in the serious and more speculative work.

'Laugh and the world laughs with you;
Weep, and you weep alone ...'

The sentiment is not necessarily true, but let us express the hope that after sharpening his wits on poems like *Continuous Creation, Extraterrestrial Intelligence, God's Highest Creation, History of the World* and *Life on Earth*, the reader will ease his scholarly neurons with an appraisal of *In the Beginning was the Word!*

For those who would prefer to be diverted by reading pieces which do not fall into any of the categories mentioned above, the questioner is happy to say that there are a number of poems about gardens, birds, father, hitch-hiking, cricket, tennis, swimming, a bullfight, classical music and so on.

Happy reading! Peace be with you!

Jonathan Pool,
Broadstairs

A BIOLOGIST'S VIEW

Jean Rostand

Who is this man who says there's no free will?
That we humans have no choice but response
To environment in all that we do.
Inheritance, he claims, predisposes
Us to behave from our genes: we react
To a circumstance and flinch when threatened;
If there is danger we respond with fear
Or take to quick heels to run away.
If this biologist's view is correct
Then we are nothing more than a harsh tune
Played by the wind and the rain – a backlash
After the whip has cracked. We're an echo
Of Nature, it seems, a mere puppy-dog
Answering the call of His Master's Voice.

ABOLITION OF RELIGION

It is with great regret that we propose
The abolition of religion. Men
Who adhere to a faith must soon dispose
Of beliefs in the cause of peace; for then

We should have less conflict. On this dear Earth
Moslems fight the Christians in the Sudan;
Arab fights Jew in Israel – not dearth
Of killing there; and in Afghanistan

All faiths, other than Islam, are exiled;
Catholic fights Protestant in Northern
Ireland; Hindu fights Buddhist in the Isle
Of Sri Lanka; the Bahai's are interned

And persecuted in Iran ... but then
These religious folk love God more than men.

A COW IS A MACHINE

I came across a comment in a book:
'A cow is a machine for making milk.'
Machine? A cow a machine? Does it look
Mechanical as it chews the cud? Silk
Worms produce silk – are they machines as well,
Built for human purposes and living
Solely to supply their needs? A small bell
Began to sound in my brain, peals giving
Thoughts of a new kind: a bicycle, a car,
An aeroplane are metallic things made
By man to be mechanical; how far
Is a cow, a worm or a man portrayed
As a machine – assembled, fitted, wrought
Automaton incapable of thought?

ALAM HALFA

Very soon after he usurped command
Of the 8th Army, nineteen forty-two,

Montgomery announced that they would stand
At Alam Halfa and halt Rommel, who
Had the British on the run. Electric
In address to senior officers,

He told them that the 8th Army would kick
The Germans out of Egypt. No offer

Of retreat. 'If we can't stay here alive,
Then let us stay here dead!' Defensive plan
For the battle: tanks hull-down, they would thrive
On Alam Halfa ridge, artillery manned,

Ready, anti-tank guns, infantry set.
They turned the tide of war, their best hour yet.

AN ENGLISH GARDEN

Munificent Earth, blessed with gardens green,
Burgeoning with flowers blue, pink and white,
Is carpeted with fine new growth, unseen
Until the rising of the morning light.
Bluebells, irises, cherry blossom too,
Splash the greensward with colour for the eye,
And newborn leaf unfolding hue on hue
Completes a scene of floral tapestry.
High above, a great globe of purest gold
Sends down its vernal largesse, light and sweet,
While we in lush arbours rest, smile and fold
Back our books to glory in the heat.
Long may we linger in this lovely place
While to the sun we turn a kindred face.

AN IMMORTAL KISS

I remember as a youth being intrigued
By a girl's kiss at a party and rather
Delighted by its bestowal and anxious
To know precisely what had happened to me,
In pursuit of a useful piece of knowledge
I consulted a dictionary to look
For meaning. What is a kiss? What did the Good
Book have to say? Eagerly I turned to 'K'

And with amusement read the immortal words:
'An anatomical juxtaposition
Of two obicularis oris muscles
In a state of contraction.' I am deeply

Indebted to this dear girl for putting me
On the path of ultra-romantic learning.

ANNUAL SWIMMER

A lady who is sixty in the town
Bathes in the sea every day: to the beach
She goes in her sandals and dressing gown,

Towel over her arm, disrobes in reach
Of the shore and wades in. Summer to spring
She takes her healthful dip near the harbour,

Turns about and uses breaststroke to bring
Her bravely back to complete her venture.
This hardy lady with body of steel

Takes a salt-sea outing all long year round,
A lone figure on winter's sad sand, chill
Wind cutting the breath in frozen, ice-bound

Weather, and she breaches the freezing sea
After breakfast cornflakes and cup of tea.

ANT INVASION

Ants in the kitchen ... coming from the wall
Cavity, I presume. No sign of nest
Outside but traced to a minute crack west
Of the door. In they come, their first scouts, all

Intent on foraging for something sweet
And appetising, and I gather three
Up in a dish, and throw them out ... I'm free
From invasions. Next night, on eager feet,

They come again, more this time, and I show
Them the window as before, believing
That the message must soon reach the thieving
Lord Ant that our kitchen has a no-go

Sign. He does not respond or give me peace ...
And each night now commando raids increase.

A PRAYER FOR DUNBLANE

We are the last, lost creatures of the sun,
Lion lords of earth, self-appointed kings
Of creation in whom, we divine, rings
The song of God; but like children we run
In the nursery in His light and gun
Our enemies – wound, weep, until death brings
Peace, while day by day His white-doved light wings
Comfort to our eyes and gives benediction.

Then pray: Our Father which in Heaven art,
Shine more clearly on those who do not feel
Thy touch; Son of God, Maker of all breath,
Give to them in shadows warmth from thy heart:
Wean thy warring people to become leal
Men; Light of the world, bless them in their death.

AT GEILO

We were having lessons in the cold snow
On the mountain slope, learning how to ski:
English folk in Norway trying to go

Downhill without losing balance in free
Fall. Arne and Steiner were astonished
At the knocks we took, the stumbles we made:

Bodies littering the run, admonished
By laughing friends who themselves were soon splayed
About, arms, legs, sticks and skis in a mess,
Some stuck until released, then up again

To the crest, sidestepping as taught. "God bless
Us!" said Arne, thinking of all the pain
We suffered, for they lived on skis since birth ...
They did not fall and loved our hardy mirth.

AUDREY AND THE SEAGULL – 1

Audrey awoke at seven and went down
To make the tea: kettle and fresh water
On the stove to boil; in slippers and gown

Went into the garden for a saunter
Across the dew-fed lawn, tipped the tea leaves
Under her red rose-bush, made to return

To her sea-girt house. From her holm-oak trees
A gull swooped down and dived at her auburn
Hair. In alarm she fell near the rose-bush

On her knees. Aggressively the grey-white
Bird circled round and with a sweeping rush
Of wide wings attacked again. In her fright

Audrey rolled beneath the bush and despaired ...
And there she lay till the gull disappeared.

AUDREY AND THE SEAGULL – 2

Wet with morning dew Audrey lay quite still,
The sky seemed clear but she was mortified
That the menace would return, so she cried
For her husband to help her. She felt chill

In the seaside air but was yet afraid
To move and called for her husband again.
In their room upstairs in oblivion
He slept, unaware that a gull had made

Vicious assaults on his beloved spouse.
At last, bravely, with teapot still in hand,
Audrey rose up, dashed across the wet land
And sought sanctuary in her own dear house.

When she woke him at seven thirty-three
He said, "You've been a long time with that tea!"

A YOUNG IRISHMAN

I remember when I was but a boy
Living in a flat in Chatteris Square,

A young Irishman, a hobbledehoy,
Knocked and Mother went to see who was there.
In an overcoat, dark, red in the face,
And hungry, he asked for something to eat.

Mother told him to wait, he knew his place,
And stood obediently with his feet

Beyond the step. She gave him bread and jam
Which he began to bite upon, sixpence
In his hand. "Missus, I thank you. I am
Looking for work but I can't get none, hence

The begging." And he came another day ...
Got sixpence more to help him on his way.

BAD DREAMS

Why do we dream as we so often do?
A long succession of vivid pictures
That ramble on in a colourful hue,
Dwelling on unhappy states and strictures
Which condemn us to feel the misery
Of former times again. I wish to change
Sleep's punishment to sweeter reverie
And dream, if I have to dream, not of strange,
Painful events but of happier things
That bring content. Then on waking I can
Smile and say that I have slept well. Heart sings
With light of morning when the mind is fresh
And free from the bars of night's darkling mesh.

BARD UNGUESSED AT

Whence comes this idea of a dramatist
Who does not reveal himself with his pen?
Those who sustain this view should not insist
In the light of new evidence, for then
Daylight would show on almost every page
The mettle of him who, in Arnold's phrase,
'Art still out-topping knowledge'. Let us rage
Against the thought that 'he's unguessed at'. Haze
Has cleared since Matthew penned his doubtful word;
Scholarship shows 'Shakespeare Identified'
In Edward de Vere. It would be absurd
To argue that his stature be denied.
This Earl who wrote, produced his courtly plays,
Reveals himself in many subtle ways.

BATMAN

I spoke to a young fellow once who told
Me that when he was in his teens he loved
To watch Batman on the box; he was bold
In his flight through the air and used to move
Like a brave, young eagle. Batman took hold

Of his imagination; he began
To believe that he also could enfold
His arms across a deep, strong chest and, man
That he was, fling both wings wide, launch and fly
Through the air. In this surreal state of mind

He went up to his room and pushed aside
The window, stood on the sill, then quite blind
To reality, jumped like a daft crow
And broke his leg in the garden below.

BEACH BALL

A journey to the beach one autumn day
With Helen and her children, five and two:
An outing on the sands to run and play
With beach ball coloured beautifully blue.

The tide fast ebbing, western wind offshore,
The sphere so light and bouncy in their spree
When, gust on gust, the ball rose off the floor
And took itself defiantly to sea.

Young Helen chased it wind-blown down the beach,
Believing she could catch its sunlit gloss
Still spinning blue to seaward out of reach –
The children howled, lamenting their bright loss.

She shrugged and said, "Adieu! Oh, what mischance!
It's gone to poor, poor children out in France!"

BEACHCOMBER

Alone in Viking Bay one summer morn
She shuffles slow and crablike to the sea;
Her head down-bent, she listens on her phone,
Her eyes alert and watching endlessly.

The tide has left the beach beswept and clean
For plunder with her black detector gear;
She skims across the dunes as though she'd glean
Where others sowed the seed another year.

She hovers like a hunter by its prey
And probes the shore with digger in her hand,
To scrabble up the coins of yesterday
That people lost while playing on the sand.
She tucks into her belt what she has found;
An hour's work has brought her thirteen pound.

BEAUTIFUL BROADSTAIRS

Beautiful Broadstairs, Mother of the Isle,
Home to those with salt-blue sea in their blood,
Nurtures her dear children, presents her brood

With sea-gifts, sea-winds and sunshine the while.
With broad, cliff promenades, ramparts of chalk,
Her husbandry delivers fields of sand

Whereon her sons may besport themselves and
Revel in her bounties where'er they walk.
With warm arms, motherly embrace, she calls
To children living in the land to be

Guests in her bright demesne, her family
Home a haven where the lone footstep falls.
A lovely place, a refuge without tears ...
I love it so; my tenure forty years.

BEEFSTEAK, QUAIL AND CLARET

I read with disquiet a résumé
Of the philosophy of George Berkeley,
Who wrote in an extraordinary way
That the material world of house, tree,
Rock, river, indeed all wonderful things
That make this beautiful world are ideas,
Sensations God puts in our minds. Sense rings
The bell of disbelief and calls up fears

For his sanity; yet this daft notion
Has won him acclaim and a place in books.
Set him adrift in the deepest ocean
To face reality or clown his looks.
I'm sure he did not hesitate to dine
On beefsteak, quail and claret for his wine!

BIG BANG

And in the beginning was the Big Bang
Some fifteen thousand million years ago
When, according to the theory, matter
Came into being, exploded and set
Off on its trip into space. Bits, pieces,
Fragments, debris, all blown apart, leaving,
One would think, a very big, empty hole
In the place where the first Big Bang began?
Somewhere in the universe there must be
A huge, immeasurably enormous,
Vast region of space with nothing in it!
Why has this space not been identified?
Unless, of course, Hoyle's theory catches light
And Continuous Creation is right.

BIRD IN THE ROWAN TREE

There is a bird up in the rowan tree
And how he sings when evening twilight falls!
His cheerful song peals out in symmetry
And my soul lifts – O listen to his calls!

A song so rich in texture that its trills
Come bubbling forth like some melodious cream
Inlaced with rippling, ever-rolling rills
Like freshets running in a summer stream.

This little bird must have a merry heart
Which bleeds anew with cadence pure and strong;
His contest is unequalled in each part,
His music score is varied, subtle, long.

A listener can no other be but glad,
Nor can its voice be ever mute or sad.

BOY WITH THREE FATHERS – 1

New like the rest he had unruly hair,
School uniform, clean shirt and red tie.
I had to write a register: "Name? Where
Do you live?" Do it neatly to get by

The Head's scrutiny. In turn the boy came
To my desk and to questions he supplied
Answers. His blue, record card was next, same
Kind of thing but details were required

Of parents, family and kin. Was he
An only child or did he have brothers
And sisters? "Mother's name?" He said, "Mary."
I wrote 'Mary', then I had some bother:

"And your father's name?" thinking it was done;
He paused a bit, half-smiled and said, "Which one?"

BOY WITH THREE FATHERS – 2

The small boy's voice was soft, no child had heard ...
A stunning moment strangely distorted;
He seemed insolent but the pupil's word
Was sincere; although I still retorted,

"How many fathers have you got?" He said,
"Three!" Briefly I pictured a merry house
With dads coming and going and the bed
Hardly empty; but I had to think, rouse

Up wits to save the boy embarrassment;
Which of three men was the boy's real father?
Intuition led me on and I meant
Well – "Which one do you like best?" And rather

Pleased he replied, "Oh, Jim, sir! He's the best!"
I wrote 'Jim' on the card, not Mary's guests.

BROADSTAIRS CARNIVAL

Down the street they came in long procession,
Colour, music and dancing for the crowd ...

On their new thrones the Beauty Queens, who bowed
Gently to us as they made progression
To the sea. Squads of brisk, youthful cadets

Marching uniformly in stiff blue ranks,
Eyes in front, stern in public gaze, past banks
Of onlookers who clap the majorettes
Following, arms aloft, high-stepping, heads

So young, it seems. Engines, cars, vans and floats
Crammed with merriment roll by, some in boats
For nautical themes; and laughing clowns lead
The play of this year's summer festival –
'Pennies in the bucket for carnival!'

BULLFIGHT – CORRIDA

In Madrid at the ancient corrida
Held in its magnificent bullfight ring,
We joined the aficionados watching
The brave toreros and braver leader,
The matador, so slender in his gold
Suit of lights; and when the President made
A signal the paso doble was played
For the majestic procession – proud, bold

Men who were to run the bulls, in the end
To kill them; the goading with the lance, pica,
Fixing of the darts, the banderillas,
Cape work, veronicas, by men who bend

The fierce creatures to their courageous will
Before they thrust the blade and make the kill.

BY HIM THE WORLD IS MADE

And do we not depend on other hands
To tend our homes, our gardens and our lives?
We need the artisan when he contrives
To build, to plumb, to paint with cleaner bands

The heady gable, mend the leaking roof,
Clear the gutter choked with leaf and rubble,
Vent the steam when boilers sing and bubble,
While we who wait on them remain aloof.

When doors don't hang and hinges clog with rust,
When engines seize and motorists are fraught,
How we lament the useless things we're taught
And give the man the treasure of our trust!

With bag of tools a man who loves his trade
Parades his worth – by him the world is made.

CAIAPHAS, HIGH PRIEST OF THE SANHEDRIN

Mea culpa! This is my guilt! Oh God,
I should have waited, I should have listened ...
A prophet, Son of Man, to one christened

Jesus, but sent Him to be scourged with rod
And whip before crucifixion. His mind
Ran counter to the Law of Moses; I
Could have asked Him again: authority?
From whence it came? But as an old Jew blind

To new truth in His light, I rent my robe
In sharp response to sacrilege; He claimed

To be one with the Godhead; I now blame
Myself for His young death and the spear's probe.
We could have talked of the Heaven above
And my place in it if I'd thought of love.

CAPSIZE

The racing was on, we tacked to the Knoll,
Heading inshore 'gainst a south-eastern breeze;
Sad to relate I was last in the scroll,
Tail of the fleet, the rest sailing with ease.
Nearer the Knoll with our backs to the sea,
Ready to turn as the others had done ...

A steamer passed by, its bow wave ran free,
A swelling tsunami rising as one.

It hit us beam-on, it tossed us up high,
Rolling the yacht like a toy in the deep;
Thrown, crew and I, plunging into the tide,
Mast broken, sails shredded – damage was steep.

Washed up on the shore, disconsolate pair,
Crowds on the beach all beginning to stare.

CHANDOGYA UPANISHAD
Book Six, VI, ii.

The Big Bang Theory of the formation
Of the Universe some fifteen thousand,
Million years ago is not as modern
Or as new as many astronomers
Would believe. No doubt the notion is based
On empirical evidence which they
Support, but it seems that the theory
Was advanced in India before Christ.
Hindu philosophers speculated
That in the beginning this Universe
Was Not-Being only; from Not-Being
Being was born! An enquiry was made:
'How could Being be born from Not-Being?'
The same question should be answered today.

CHILDREN OF THE STREET

O, how we played as children of the street!
Each season brought its happy round of games:
From morn till eve, 'less it was raining, fleet
Of foot, for hours we flew paper planes

We had made and watched them glide forty yards!
With glass-coloured marbles we competed,
Lost and won, took our treasure home; at cards
We ran 'matchstick pontoon 'till defeated,

Then turned to cannon, cricket, football, skates,
Were pirates with Jimmy Maynard who taught
Us how to fence with slender sticks, mates
Formed into a gang, musketeers we thought.

Dear Jimmy, older, wiser, led us well,
We respected him, played the game like hell.

CHOIR PRACTICE

O, how we sang together on Friday
Eve, women and men: sopranos, altos,
Tenors, basses, all standing in massed ranks,

Sharing scores, blissful as the music goes
Into hearts and minds, lifting us to Heaven.
Music was our glory and not the least,
For we sang John Ireland's *These Things Shall Be.*

As well as *Hiawatha's Wedding Feast.*
Fauré's R*equiem* was a lovely work,
So moving in the soft tones we rehearsed.

Doc. Thomas also ran the college Small
Choir and Madrigal Group – we were deep versed
In music and I sang in choirs three.
Beauteous things these lovely sounds will be.

CLOUDS

Beset with winter greys I miss the clouds
Of summer on their voyage in the blue;
Full-rigged fore and aft, bellied, without shrouds,

They hold their fullness till the wind is due.
Sure and sailing in golden fleets of white,
They glide across the deep like crested swans,

Serene and calm, unhurried as the night
Which lowers when its darker mantle dons.
When armadas come, cumulus by name,

Banked and breasted on mountain's highest peak,
Their beauty is above our earthen frame,
They are the little Heaven mortals seek.
But where are they when winter settles hard
And icicles develop in the yard?

COMPOSERS AND MUSICIANS

What is our debt to a fine composer
Of music who gives his soul to the world?
The lovely sound he creates reposes

In our clear memory's hearing; unfurled
It is brought forth again to be reheard
And loved once more. The musician who makes

Such exquisite sound is like a rare bird
Singing at the window, notes which will take
Wing and live. He hears a piece that is new,

Transfers it to manuscript with a pen
For others to play, and our delight, few
Giving joy to many. To such rare men,

Composers, musicians, all, we give praise;
Their talent will uplift us all our days.

CONSTELLATIONS

How beautiful the stars, their cold-steel light
Sharp as a sword when winter's frozen hard;
The dark, frosted sky patterned like a card,
Canis Minor and Major to the right.
These age-old constellations cut the sky

With blue-white stones that sparkle as a set
Of sapphires, precious to behold, a net-
Work of beauty in all its panoply.

Great Orion, a signpost in the east,
With Betelgeuse and Rigel at its points,
Leads down to Sirius whose light anoints
The Earth most strongly with its starry feast.

Long may silver stars keep their olden place
In Heaven and give warmth to winter's face.

CONTINUOUS CREATION

Theories abound and men who think they know,
Who scan all space with Hubble's telescope,
Say the Universe was formed long ago,
Some fifteen thousand million years. They hope
To persuade us a singular Big Bang
Created all matter from nothing, sent
It soaring into space at speeds, which hang
Credulity by the neck. Reason went.
It seems we must not ask what came before
The Big Bang. We must not question or think
Those thoughts which upset the theory. Abhor
This nonsense – reason goes beyond the brink
And instead considers with elation
Hoyle's thought – Continuous Creation.

CROUPIER

Hands held on a cloth of green; and her hands
Tender as the vine, still strong in their root
And resilience. Alone the Queen stands,

Lithe as the panther-palmist, her four suits
Passing to and fro in short, sequence runs,
Dispensing eight, ten, Jack, King, the digits

Rising to a limit of twenty-ones.
In the quiet room where players fidget
In an anxiety of twilight fear,

She deals justice and injustice apart
From guess, gamble, twist, stick of those who dare
To break her. Sadly the losers depart,

Leaving her Queen of amber light and shade
From whom fortune in cards is never made.

DANCING LESSON

He came to give us lessons, sixpence each,
An evening's royal pleasure with a smile,
And at the club with partners he would teach
Us how to dance the latest ballroom style.

The hold with hands, my arm about her waist,
Her left upon my upper arm, so neat,

Our heads held up, her head correctly placed
To make her look a Queen with regal feet.

And left foot leading, so her right withdraws,
A ballroom stride that moves the lady on,
And two as one with rhythm's grace, no flaws,
In motion to the waltz's triple tone.

A social grace, well taught, that will enhance
A lady's love of gentlemen who dance.

DANCING PARTNER

I met a lady in a Paul Jones, put
An arm about her and made to advance
With the left; like a stone her golden foot
Remained fast; she didn't know how to dance

The first, basic steps of the Snowball Waltz.
Using shoulders and arms I made to shove

Her along, feet well back, dodging her false
Tread, swung a natural turn, but my dove
Would not go round. She went on in a line,
Her black, matron's dress shining in the light

As we came to the band. A half incline
Was needed then and I tried hard, a bright

Forced smile of joy as I tugged her right hand ...
She hit a saxophone and wrecked the stand.

DASHING WHITE SERGEANT

Names of folk dances like The Dashing White
Sergeant are as lovely as the dances
Are themselves. Whoever had the insight

To choose that elegant name enhances
The joy we have in the figure of eight

When we weave back to back with the ladies,
Link hands and advance in ranks with a great
Shout of glee. What pleasure when the parade

Is under way and we make sets in haste
For The Cumberland Square Eight, a charming

Group of four, young pairs, arms round slender waists,
The lightest touch, eyes and smiles disarming.
Do not sit out. Come, make up sets and dance!
The spirit shines as Nature's reels advance.

DAVID AND PAUL
(24th June 2001)

On perhaps the hottest day of the year
The Handicap Final was being played
At the club: David's attempt, hotly made,
To beat Paul, the number one seed, and bear

The trophy away, both remaining deep
Behind the base line and exchanging shot
In rallies long and wearing. David got
His returns in but he was wont to keep
Back too often. In the heat he tired,
Sweated, became exhausted, bent his brow
To rest. Winning nine games to seven, now
The end was in sight but though he fired

Himself on he had to concede the match
Which his friends had been so concerned to watch.

DEAR MOTHER

Dear mother made the dust fly with her brooms
When April came and warmth was in the air;
She shook the curtains from their winter rooms
And scrubbed the rise and fall upon the stair.
Old carpets strung out on the garden line
For punishment, to let loose all their dust,
With beatings sore they trembled like the vine
That rattles so when March winds blow as must.
And blankets too were shaken by the ear,
And cupboards cleaned and emptied of their store
Which nourished us in winter's hemisphere
When ice is cold and frost is sharp and hoar.
What labour when the sun heats up the earth
And mother bends her back to show her worth!

DEATH OF LITERATURE

Seated at the huge, brown desk in her room
At college, a desk built up on a dais,
Miss Jenkins waged war with many a boom,

Boom against the students who had to face
Her verbal onslaughts. Red-lipped, black-headed,
A clever woman, no doubt, she brandished

Speech like a sharp, bright sword and we dreaded
Harangues when with flashing eyes she vanquished
All her foes. One fine, Saturday morning

On a timetable change our English class
Was despatched to her room where she, scorning
A sky-blue, sunny day, talked, talked, talked past

Decency for a weary, double hour
While she slaughtered literature from her bower.

DIGGING DRAINS

One summer I had a job digging drains.
A student needing money could not choose

But find work those days. Foreman Mr Hughes,
A dour, laconic man, was not at pains
To say much but took me to the new site

Of a half-built, brick house, gave me a spade
And said to dig a drain soon to be laid
From the side kitchen to the road. Not slight
But tall, the bending in that blazing sun

Burnt me dry. It was a heavy, blue clay
Underfoot, packed hard as glue, and all day
It resisted. By lunch I ached like one

In misery, arms leaden, back half bent,
Bruised, scorched, sore and weary ... till homeward went.

DINING ALONE

How people can eat their dinner and talk
While doing so, I cannot comprehend.

Eating hot roast is a delicate task
Which should not give offence to any friend
At table. If we reverse the process
And to a man who wants to make a speech

Present lunch and say to him, "Eat!" I guess
He would protest and be indignant each

Time the ploy is mentioned; yet the same cove
Will eat pork pie, masticate and chatter
Without thought. I feel sure we could improve
Table manners if we said the platter

Comes first, talk later, excusing the bone.
To be candid I'd rather dine alone.

DINOSAURS

One hundred and seventy million years
Ago, the dinosaurs who ruled the earth

Were hideous to behold and their worth
Was in doubt. Monstrous, bulkier than bears,

Manifestations of evolution
That had gone wrong, they were gruesome beyond

Belief, ugly, loathsome, needing a wand
To waft them off the earth. The solution

Came with time and these gigantic errors
In the scheme of life happily faded,

Making way for other forms less jaded,
Of a smaller kind – the birds with feathers.

I'd sooner see a thrush go flying by
Than pterodactyls blackening the sky.

DOCTOR IN CALLIS COURT ROAD – 1

Called from his bed at a quarter to two,
Summoned from sleeping when sleeping is due,
He answers the telephone, head quite numb,
Appeal from the breast of a working mum.

"A cut on the head and his breathing's slow;
He fell down the stairs and I'm worried so."
"I'll come," says the Doctor. "Just keep him warm.
And where did you say that he'd hurt his arm?"

The Doctor's head is heavy with slumber ...
"In Maynard Street? And what is the number?"
A huddle of bedclothes left behind him,
Dresses again, no need to remind him
Of winter's blast or of frost's sharp biting
In streets half black with their dim-wick lighting.

DOCTOR IN CALLIS COURT ROAD – 2

Physician on call, his bag by the door,
Shivers in the porch and goes to the car.
In Maynard Street where the hallway is bright,
A house still lit on a Saturday night,

Mother is waiting, on watch by the door,
Wrapped in a dressing gown, beer on the floor.
"Where is the patient?" he asks when he comes;
She leads up the stairs – O dutiful mums!

A youth stiff-drunk is asleep on the bed,
Oozing fresh blood from a gash on the head;
Radial fracture when falling downstairs
And a damaged knee with ligament tears.
The Doctor waits till the ambulance comes,
Sipping hot coffee with one of his mums.

DOCTOR IN CALLIS COURT ROAD – 3

He has strapped up the arm to hold it fast,
And patched up his head with Elastoplast,
Dispatches the youth for hospital care
And accepts her thanks for sending him there.

At home once again he tramps up the stairs,
Undresses again and crawls into bed,
Rests his cheek on a Slumberland pillow,
Hoping with hope that the telephone's dead.

His eyelids are closing with sleep which brings
Comfort and ease to a head that is numb ...
At quarter to three the telephone rings ...
("Oh God!") says the Doctor, "Of course, I'll come."
The poor man's head is heavy with slumber ...
"In Welbeck Street? And what is the number?"

DOMESTIC VIOLENCE

How did she bear the rages of this man,
This drunken sot to whom she early wed?
His insults, gibes and tantrums which began
When whisky fumes assailed his crimson head?
Rage-driven by the bottle he'd assault
The woman who had borne him dual heirs
And beat her with his fists for little fault
Then punch her face and push her down the stairs.

This evil wretch, this bully of the night,
Complaining of a woman's coloured braid,
A tyrant and a coward in his fight
Against a wife whose love had never strayed.
And then at last her happiness to prove,
She left the brute and found a better love.

DOWN THE MIDDLE

It was time for tennis on Monday eve,
Men's four, a game we all try hard to win.
I spun a racket, lost, we would receive
Service from Peter with his wristy spin.
Two surgeons playing at the other end,
Big hitters both and fearful with their strokes
'Gainst John and I, two Johns, and they would send
Us home miserable like poor, dull mokes
Who can't score. John said, "Let's return their shots
Down the middle. Perhaps they'll hesitate
Or leave the ball to the other man." Lots
Of points we won this way and it was late
When we finished; the light had gone above;
The two Johns were smiling – two sets to love!

'DO YOU WALK MUCH?'

A tournament at the club, seven rounds
To be played with partners, each round of nine
Games, four until noon when the lunch bell sounds

In the pavilion: chicken, salad, wine,
Sweet, coffee served for all. P.M. three more
Rounds to complete the event. Good weather

Favoured play but friend, Anne, was stiff and sore
Next day from exertion, her new, feather
Hat would be a burden. An appointment

With the doctor was due to check on blood
Pressure. "Do you walk much?" He clearly meant
To encourage more exercise. Anne stood

Up. "No, but I have just played sixty-three
Games of tennis! That's good enough for me."

DREAM THAT WOULD NEVER FADE

The boy, resident in a children's home,
Attended school in clothing blue and grey.

An orphan in spirit he would soon come
To be allied with friends, masters by day.
An essay to be written in his class,
'A Dream', it was a subject he would keep

In his heart, a memory to surpass
Dream recall: the playground was a sea, deep

As an ocean; in it he was swimming
Alone, peering through the glass of the hall
Where the boys stood in prayer, water brimming
To the roof outside. He wanted to fall

In line with his friends, friends with whom he played ...
And when he woke, the dream would never fade.

DRILLING CHEEK TO CHEEK

Good-looking for a dentist, that's the truth,
And working on a molar upper left,
The drill was angled upward in the tooth

And she was crouching right of me, not deft.
The drill seemed heavy, maiden's fist was slight,
She paused, inspected, started up afresh,

Then peered into my mouth with hand-held light
And changed the drill head for a smaller mesh.
"Oh, this is better!" said she, drilling on ...

The bit was buzzing saw-like in my head,
And chatting now, all hesitation gone,
Her hair was on my chest while I was led
To choke – "Ugh! Ugh!" for I had felt a tweak ...
She'd drilled right through the molar to the cheek!

DR KASIRI AT EVENING TENNIS

Medical friend, surgeon, born in Iran,
Naturalised, respected, skilled in the art
Of Orthopaedic Surgery, takes part
In evening tennis as a doubles man.
In tandem we play whenever we can,
Weather permitting, and he with great heart,
Taking the stronger role from the game's start,
Shows his artistry to the also-ran.
Without anaesthetic they bear the pain
Of defeat when he runs, drives with power
And changes the racket for better strings.
Our friends then turn for his service again,
Knowing that he, Firuz, man of the hour,
Loves them, the game, the pleasure that it brings.

EDWARD'S COTTAGE – LAMPETER VELFREY

There he dwells, cricketing friend of my youth,
'In the sticks' – a quiet hamlet in Wales.
In other times well-travelled in pursuit

Of his copy and scientific tales:
Teacher, Science Journalist and Author
Of books on Extraterrestrial 'G',

Now 'surfing the net' on a computer
To keep up to date as he has to be.
Dark beamed, Tudor hearth and a comfy nook

It is, cushioned chairs and glowing log fires
Stacked with old timber brought down by the brook,
Home for a scholar and all he aspires.

Lover of tennis, sport in which he shone;
Not many men have played at Wimbledon.

ELECTRIC THINKING

Electric impulses generate thought
And they can be seen on MRI scan:
Glimpses of lightning from synapses fraught
With the amperage of sapient Man.

Very small impulses, milliamp size?
Smaller in charge than Electric CT,
Thoughts are aroused where intelligence lies,
Is sound of their passing never to be?

Lightning which flashes in storm-laden skies,
Thousands of volts in a cloud-breaking blaze:
God thinking hard – did the mountains arise
When forming the Earth in six solemn days?
If brains are electric, it has to be
God is the power and we are DC.

ELECTROCONVULSIVE THERAPY
An Italian Legend

He fled into the grounds and climbed the wall
Pursued by angry men in milk-white coats:
An inmate, schizophrenic, running all
The sweet way to freedom; and laughing, gloats;

But in the fields the chase grew warm and hot,
Attendants gaining on their crazy wight
Who ran in terror of the care he got;
They locked him in a cell each day and night.

He saw a pylon, cables up on high,
And climbed the bars in frenzied fear and pain,
He touched a line – a flash lit up the sky!
He fell to earth and did not move again.

The patient lived; the shock he had endured
Had eased his mind – the schizo's head was cured.

ELIZABETH II
HER GOLDEN JUBILEE, 2002

We wish to meet the Queen, make her a bow,
And compliment the Monarch on her reign.
Her fifty years as Head of State is gain
To the nation which must consider how

To hold its sovereignty. These foppish men
Who seek to federate with other lands
Do not know our homage; they tie our hands
With EC rules and regulations, then

Declare it is for profit and our good.
They should remember duty to the realm
As Her Majesty does, follow her helm
And steer a sovereign course where our blood
Is not diminished. Fealty, we relate,
Is foremost to Queen, people and the state.

ENGLISH BY DEFAULT

The world is smaller now than 'what' it was,
And 'different to' or is it 'different from'?

Do they assert the reason is 'because'
All television broadcasts have become
A model of good English for today?
So 'let's face it' just 'between you and me'

The speakers are not clear in what they say
'At this moment in time' or it may be

We stand 'shoulder to shoulder' as we must;
'I mean' 'you know', the standard is not high;
These flaws of speech are common as the dust
And 'at the end of the day' I could sigh.

So have we 'hit the nail upon the head'?
These people should be careful where they tread.

EPILEPTIC FIT

A short, strangled scream – I ran from the room
And beheld a pretty girl on the floor:

Her friend kneeling beside her like a groom
Nursing a creature in the corridor.
The girl was rigid, her white face distraught,
Her feet together in a chilling line,

Her eyes stark with fear as though she had caught
Sight of the Devil, evil and malign.

Arms stuck at her side and both her fists tight,
She shook with earth tremors, force four or five,
Heels drumming the concrete; friend who was bright
Turned her head to the left, kept her alive.

And then she relaxed – but what a sharp scream
From one so young! – so helpless did she seem.

EXTRATERRESTRIAL INTELLIGENCE

There is not much doubt that forms, modes of life
Endowed with keen intelligence exist
In the Universe today. Suns are rife

In our galaxy alone; planets blessed
With their creative light would generate
Conditions of life so prevalent here.

Imagine a civilisation great,
Much greater than our own, a thousand years
Ahead; they would not deign to touch this dark

Earth, its primitive ways, its petty wars;
Tribesman fighting tribesman, brother who marks
Down brother for death. All our killing scars

Are deep and give pain to intelligence.
They will avoid us till we have more sense.

FALLING IN THE SEA

Moored in the rising waters of the bay
Were yachts in line parading on the tide
And I had come to work on board that day,
Cleaning the ship and oiling clips that ride
In grooves – she was Bermuda rigged like most –

And needed oil to keep her running free;
The boom was resting on its cradle posts,
Its tackle creaked when we were out at sea.

Upon the transom bold I stood to tease
The pulley round – a neighbour ship came bump!
And thinking not I used a foot to ease

It off and stood astride the gap – Oh! jump
Or split? I had no choice and had to fall
In fully dressed just by the harbour wall.

FALLING IN THE THAMES

We were on a course at Bisham Abbey,
Young novices all, learning how to sail.

Dinghies on the bank under covers, pale,
Morning sunlight spilling through the far trees
And in a cold wind much talk in progress:
Hull, boom, mast, rudder, transom, halyards, shrouds,

All part of the ship – "Tiller up!" and clouds
Overhead, "Tiller down!" and for most dress

Inadequate. Three quarters of an hour
Still shivering later, covers off, fleet
Launched, crews assigned, boldly, with slippered feet
I stepped on deck – the mast hit me and "Urgh!"

I was tipped in the icy, green water
Of the Thames like a lamb to the slaughter.

FATHER'S BREAKFAST

On his day of rest, one day in seven –
As boys we rarely saw him – our Dad would
Enjoy a royal breakfast. Mother stood
By the stove until he was ready, then

When all was hot, as he liked, she would serve
A splendid meal, rich as a breakfast goes:
Eggs plural, bacon triple, tomatoes
Cooked magnificently whole to conserve

Heat, mushrooms and black sausage and fried bread,
Two pieces properly browned, scallops bought
From the fishmonger, none of which he thought
To leave, and lastly or he'd shake his head,

Garnish of fresh, green watercress over
The bacon ... and Dad would be in clover.

FEAR OF THE LORD

The beginning of wisdom is the fear
Of the Lord ... which the Bible enjoins us
To believe, in Psalms, Job, Proverbs it's clear

That awe is the basis of respect, thus
A healthy fear of God would do none harm.
If it's wise to have respect for the Lord

Then veneration should include wise, warm
Feelings for parents, teachers in accord
With police and those in authority.

Fear of God, of teachers and law is good
For youth who have to learn the hierarchy
And realise their place in line and blood.
And let them learn the sequence of the Word:
God is first, neighbour second, I am third.

FIFTH OF NOVEMBER

Until my girl and boy were in their teens
We had a party every Bonfire Night:
A guy on a pole to be burned in bright
Blue and red flames, and torches that had been

Made for the procession with muddy heels
To a huge stack of wood soon to be lit;
Sparklers, bangers, jumping crackers that flit
About, Roman Candles, Catherine Wheels,

Nailed to the side of the shed, that would spin
In circles of fire, things to remember;
Rockets to shoot each fifth of November
And spuds in silver foil to roast them in.

And when the blaze had warmed us for the night
We trooped indoors for supper in the light.

FIRE!

My son telephoned for the Fire Brigade,
Emergency, nine, nine, nine! The garage

Across the street was alight and it made
Palls of dense black smoke as an orange, large
Jet of flame from a burning motorbike
Seared up, engulfed the top, the southern side

Of the house. Fire engines came in a trice,
Men spilled out, ran hoses, broke in and tried

To find Malcolm's dog. Sadly it was laid
On the lawn, asphyxiated by smoke.
So prompt were the men that the house was saved,
But Malcolm grieved like any normal bloke.

And last we made these gallant firemen tea,
Large mugs of it, and praised their bravery.

FIRST FLIGHT

A sleek, slim craft, white and blue, would fly me
To Sicily over land, sea and Alps,

Of all high places! Could I pray for help
To see the journey through or would I be
Comforted in some other way? The seats
Were close, leg-room tight, and we were compressed

Like minnows in a long tin. Could I rest
On the flight or would the wings fall off? Feats

Of aviation are needed for first
Fliers ... and then the stewardess appeared,
So poised, calm and neat, her sweet face feared
Nothing; gently asked would I not ease thirst

With a coffee? I smiled and held my fears;
This brave, young woman had flown for eight years!

FIRST OF NOVEMBER

Two ladies swimming in an autumn sea,
A robe and sandals waiting on the sand
Where ragged waves are pounding endlessly
Upon a beach that's sunlit like the land.

Their progress hampered by a running tide,
And strokes are short and measured I can see;
Their shelter is the jetty wall beside
The fishing boats that wallow in its lee.

Emerging from the waters semi-clad,
Like Venus being born from out her shell,
They saunter to the steps berobed and glad
That we applaud their hardiness so well.

So strong they are, so warm, they do not chill,
They swim throughout the winter 'less they're ill.

FISH THAT JUMPED

Two canoes on the Thames near Maidenhead
And we were four, like Three Men In A Boat,
On the river, on holiday, all wed
To sunshine, reedy haunts, peace in remote

Streams among the aits, then the weather turned
To rain. For three days it cruelly poured
On us in two-man canoes and we spurned
Father Thames' slimy, green banks when we moored.

Of a sudden from still, grey deeps a perch
Leapt up and over the gunwale, and fell
In the cockpit at my feet. "Urgh!" I lurched
And couldn't touch its writhing body. "Help!"

I cried; and laughing, Edward paddled near,
Leaned over, scooped and threw it in the weir.

FOOTBALL IN THE LOUNGE

When Simon was a boy we often played
In local park or beach on any patch
We could find: soccer, cricket, throw and catch,
To hone the skills he'd need in man's parade.
In summer months we roved the garden wide,
Ruffed up the lawn with cricket bat and ball,
But when the clouds of autumn came and pall
Of night fell soon, we pulled stumps, went inside

And brought football to the lounge. Rules were strict:
The ball below knee height and strong shots barred,
Dribble, weave and feint, we'd both tackle hard
And glance off chairs to help the goals we kicked.

In all the years we played when sport was king,
We never smashed a lamp or broke a thing!

FORGETFUL SURGEON

The nurse forgot to give me the pre-med,
And grumbling said that I should be asleep!

The trolley had not come so I could keep
Appointment in theatre, so she said,
But not knowing what was wrong I would be
Late! Getting out of bed in cotton shift,

I donned a dressing gown, refused a lift,
And holding hands with nurse we ran some three

Wards along. At the door the surgeon stood,
In blue-striped shirt and braces, collar, tie,
And looking sorry made apology –
He'd brought no instruments, he said, but would

Bring them tomorrow. Then my nurse began
On our return to grumble 'cause I ran!

FORGETTING NAMES

I met a charming lady in the street,
I knew her well and she, a friend, knew me.
A rush of news and ... "How's the family?"

She asked and smiled – we did not often meet.
She told me she had passed her flying test
For pilot and instructor, gallant soul,

And qualified she taught, that was her goal,
To give her pupils aviation's best.
While we conversed my mind was in the air –

What is her name? I felt half riven, rent;
I blushed and felt acute embarrassment ...
The lapses of memory, I fear.
Why could I not remember in my need?
That evening I recalled it – late, indeed.

FORGIVE THEM, LORD, THEY KNOW NOT WHAT THEY DO

At bridge one evening with the Vicar, where
I called a heart and had to play the hand,

The points were even and I did not dare
To lose the rubber, you will understand ...
For he and I were partners at the time,
We'd had a muffin tea and ate our fill,

Then made up foursomes but no faith sublime
Could hide the truth – the Vicar's look could kill!

He saw my weakness with a kingly card
And how I ruffed when ruff was not required ...
'You stupid man!' The Vicar's jaw was hard;
I read the thought; my other heart expired.

I lost my nerve, revoked and trumped his Jack ...
And had to quote the scriptures to his back!

FORTY TO ONE

I saw an old man sitting on a bench:
Thin, grey hair, head down, body slumped, eyes glazed;
While round the corner, a hundred yards hence,

Forty men were playing bowls: voices raised
In the grand heat of play, five teams of eight,
Four against four and their woods on the green,

Surrounding the white jack in circle state
And men stooped, measuring the victory.
Forty men all dressed in the purest white

From head to toe, lively, sprightly, intent,
Most of them 'old boys', grandfathers, sound, light
Of heart, though some had ancient shoulders bent.

Say, who was alive on that golden day?
The forty or the one? How would you say?

FREEDOM OF SPEECH

Sophie, Countess of Wessex, in Dubai,
Engaged in conversation with a sheik,
Said what she thought of Government. The fake
Arab trickster sent her remarks, truly

Given, to the tabloid press and the sky
Fell in upon the Countess. Let her take
Heed; she must not speak her mind or yet break
The code of Royals or Civility.

As a child she must be seen but not heard!
Whate'er she says at any time must be
Socially correct. Freedom of address

Has gone and like a clipped and tethered bird
She dare not give utterance to her free
Thoughts nor cross masters in the gutter press.

FREE TRADE
(Smuggling)

A quiet sea in the night and no word
Ashore as the lugger sails in. A small
Boat heaves to and the cargo is transferred:
Tea for M'lord, silk for his wife and all
Her girls, brandy, wine, tobacco, white lace
For gents in London. On the mist-cold beach

Owlers hump the bales where the horses pace
To ferry the goods to market but each

Man knows danger, for Customs and Excise
Men keep guard on the coasts and remote bays
Of Kent and Sussex. Their treacherous spies
Lurk on the cliffs, paid, willing to betray

The poor folk from whom Free Trade always sprang
At the risk of their lives and those who'd hang.

FRENCH EXAM – 1

It was the last day of term and the last
Lesson of the afternoon and 1c
Had French. It was a staff joke, almost past
Belief, that this third class who could not see
The difference between a noun and verb
In English should devote their energy

To a foreign tongue. Joe would not disturb
Their intellect on the last day, so he

Said they could play their word games in English.
A little girl spoke – "Sir, we haven't had
A French exam!" Joe, who'd not extinguish
Such zest, hurriedly gave out papers, sad
To reflect on a dubious exam
And reports for this class. Quietly – "Damn!"

FRENCH EXAM – 2

There was little time that last afternoon
For finesse or deep learning. "Write your name
On the map of France on your desk as soon
As you can." A great fuss with their pens, same
As usual. "Pens down!" Joe collected
The papers. The little girl said, "Have we

Finished?" ... "Yes, do your word games." He sifted
The maps into three: those that were clearly
Right way up – A; those with France on its side –
B; and those that were upside down, marked C.
Joe still had reports to write and the tide
Was ebbing fast. 1c were pleased and he

Wished them, "*Au revoir, mes enfants!*" now glad
The little girl remembered when she had.

GALATEA

I seek a love who's cast in silent stone,
Who's seen in Art's most lovely tint and trace,
Who passes in some solitary place
The long hours of melancholy – alone
She waits. O cold and stone-like beauty find
The one who is to give to thee breath's life
And make of thee a well-beloved wife
Living as yet an image in his mind:
By him create in purest, female form,
Free from mar or fault or Maker's blunder,
Perfect and strong, envisaged as a warm
And living Galatea. Though thou wonder
At the impeding sloth of time's slow storm,
Fear not! we shall ne'er be kept asunder.

GLOVES

In the deeps of winter Father would wear
A thick, wind-proof, grey, Crombie overcoat
When he went outdoors and a trilby hat
Above a woollen scarf to keep him warm.

No matter what the icy temperature
He seemed very well clad and would not dote
On vile weather, preferring summer heat.
Strangely, and it never did him much harm,

He declined to wear gloves. No snow would dare
Make him relent and his hands, rough as oats,
Would ride in pockets or accept storm beats
And blasts with usual, stoical charm.

I thought it strange, this weather-fingered stand,
But I don't wear gloves on a winter hand.

GOD'S HIGHEST CREATION

I have never seen Venus sweeping roads

Or digging for coal in a deep, wet mine,
Climbing a pylon whose spark overloads

Or mending a roof where the hips incline.
They do not build bridges, houses or flats,
Saw timber, catch cod or load heavy drays,

But oh! They look gorgeous in Ascot hats
And how they excel in ladylike ways!

If I were ill in a hospital ward,
I'm sure to respond to a nurse's touch,
And when sons are born I would soon be bored

If mothers were men – it would be too much!
Ladies, be true and live with elation;

You are on Earth God's highest creation.

GOD TOOK DEAR RICHARD

A friend rang; he had awful news to tell:
My dear friend, Richard Wilson, had just died.
A sudden heart attack, we thought him well,
His coffee on the table at his side.

His wife came breezing in and found him dead,
Slumped in his chair, his hand upon his chest,
And shocked, stunned, stupefied she bent her head –
It was the onset of no sleep, no rest.

At this dread news I found I could not speak;
The shock I felt o'erwhelming, far too great;
My student, brother-colleague at his peak –
So young! I thought him young – just fifty-eight.

God took dear Richard – he was in his prime!
I grieve, grieve, and remember all the time.

GOING TO TAUNTON – 1

We were hitch-hiking west, Roy, Ted and I,
Three six-footers on the road and thumbing
For a lift on the march, cars passing by

In the heat of noon, but none were coming
Near us. Traffic was light that summer day,
But unconcerned we went on, believing
That we should be seen walking on our way,

Not idling at the roadside, achieving
Nothing. In shorts and shirt, with small packs light
To carry, we soldiered on till it hit

Our dull minds that we were too many. "Right,
Roy, go with Ted to Taunton – we must split
Up." Saying farewell to brother and friend
I went alone to see how I would fend.

GOING TO TAUNTON – 2

Striding down a country road and turning
When I heard the sound of cars from the east,
I raised a hand to court a lift, yearning
To reach Taunton first. A shooting-brake passed,
Then stopped ahead and I hurried to board
It. A weather-bronzed man in a brown hat

Told me to get in. "Thank you," I said. Bored
With his lonely journey we had a chat

And he was glad of company. A street
In town and he asked for a helping hand.

In the brake, beneath a grey canvas sheet
That I had seen but didn't understand,
Lay a dead, mangy sheep! I swallowed hard –
I had to hump it to the knacker's yard!

GOLDEN TREASURY

I read The Golden Treasury all through
To harvest works I could esteem, admire,
And soon I heard clear notes that were like new
Sounds of music, word songs that would aspire

To be remembered. I heard the voice
Of Keats, Brooke, Yeats, Binyon and Tennyson,
And read their odes to those who would rejoice
In their fame. I loved G. K. Chesterton's

Before the Roman came to Rye ... delight
In humoured rhyme. Two works of De la Mare,
Trees, Arabia, are not his best, bright
Star though he is; but of poems so fair

To find, to read and devour, I herald
The *Omar Khayyam* of E. Fitzgerald.

GOVERNORS' MEETING

The meeting was in progress when I walked
Down to collect a paper from the room.
The Governors were there and how they talked

Endlessly, including the Head, for whom
I felt sympathy when he faced the Chair.
But this day something was amiss; the door
Stood open and two legs and feet, a pair,
Extended from a body on the floor.

I hastened in – the Head had had a stroke!
Eyes open, bleeding from the nose, he lay

Supine, trying to wave them on. I spoke
Sharply – "The meeting's closed!" But, by God! they
Protested! They had let the Head fall down
And bleed! The stupidity of such clowns!

GULL GLIDE

White bodied, wings spread wide and hanging there
On the heeling wind, he skims the steep, grey
Rim of the cliff, banks seaward and dives where
The bay burns in the sun; curve of flight may
Bring him round again, looping on the wind
Which cuts the shore, coasting on the uplift
Like a soft-sounding glider that is pinned
To sky in a feather-fine, full-flown drift
Of hidden power. What God-given force
Keeps him there, moves him and lets him gull-glide
While I watch the mystery of life's course
Uncomprehending as the turn of tide?
If I could fly on wings as strong and white,
Would I declare the joy of seagull flight?

GUNNER BERT

The gunner had broken camp and got drunk
In Tampin. Soon brought back under arrest
And locked in the guardroom, he fell and sank

Into a moist sleep. The next day his best
Defence in front of the CO was 'Thirst!'
In a tropical climate this was true,

But the Colonel was not amused. Bert's first
Offence got fourteen days' hard labour, two
Weeks in the glasshouse and his head was shaved!

This upset Bert; 'mid his protestations
He argued that his blond hair should be saved –
It was against army regulations.

I had to guard him once while he sweated
In the gym with a rifle overhead.

GUT FELLOWS

How are these heaving mountains made of pork?
These rolling hills of flesh on stumpy paws?
They grunt and squeal in grotesque, pigsty talk
And wallow in the mud-wet out of doors.

Atrocious eaters of the slush and waste
Which we refuse, they shake with gutful coughs
And seem to lack the rudiments of taste
When rooting in the swill of farmyard troughs.

Bristled, pink and ugly, their name is used
For slander: 'You pig! Fat swine!' and 'Road hog!'
In the hate-stream of language so abused
Are they, as their unhappy cousin, dog.

Hardly the thing to rave about in rhyme –
Bale-eyed, belly-wet, mucky all the time.

HALLMARKS ON A SPOON

"I'd sooner bake a cake than read a book,"
She said, a lady who lives in a fine,
New house, her grand piano in a nook
In the lounge, with pictures, objects that shine
With love. She buys silver-ware, has a fond

Understanding of hallmarks on a spoon,
Can recognise a theme from the second
Symphony of Rachmaninov as soon
As I hum it and seems, at the first take,
A woman of culture and high degree.

Books are not of her world; nor would they make
Her more able than she appears to be.

This serene lady with a mixing bowl
Is, I would say, a more practical soul.

HEADMASTER HILL

Once each week after school prayers Mr Hill
Led us in singing. All masters dismissed
Except Mr Fox, piano, we'd fill
The Albert Hall with our voices, nor Liszt
Could have been more rhapsodic, for the Head
Endeavoured to uplift our rough, boyish
Souls with stirring music. Mr Fox, wed
To his piano, played with great flourish
And bravura and we sang till the hall
Shook: *Old Father Thames, Glorious Devon,*
The Floral Dance, Rule Britannia, all
These songs held our hearts but *Jerusalem*
Was golden, so we rehearsed it again
And again – and sang for our music men!

HE COULD NOT READ

I was new to the school and had 4G
For English, a disparate class of boys,
Girls aged fourteen or so who would not be
Oxford academics. For them the joys
Of life were limited by upbringing,
Inheritance, genes and ability,

But we got on nicely; they like acting
Plays, taking parts and being somebody
Else. One day soon a boy named Ronnie Star,
A dour lad with a flat, serious mien,
Approached and said, "My brother, Gerry Star,
Is twelve. He can read, sir, but I'm fourteen

And I can't." His eyes fell, his pale face sad ...
I cheered him up, he smiled, our friendship glad.

HISTORY AT BROADSTAIRS

The most beautiful beach of sea-washed sand,
Ringed by ancient cliffs of chalk topped with grass,
Curves in the sunlight below the headland

To an old harbour where lobster-smacks pass
When garnering the salt sea. Dickens stopped
Here and summered in Bleak House; the young Queen

Slept in the white Town Hall; Thirty-nine steps
In the cliff go down to where the tide's been
Lapping at the base; and author Defoe,

Who came here in seventeen twenty-three,
In his report said that he didn't know
How local men earned their bread; they were free

With their time, smugglers all, and moved him on,
Happy in free trade when Old Dan had gone.

HISTORY OF THE WORLD

Where is the use to tell of English Kings
And Queens, a battle, a plot and a war,
Uprisings, repression? Such tales do bring

Perspective, but an island's insular,
A fraction of the globe; we need to know
Of the whole Earth and of progress that speeds

The lives of all people both high and low:
Tales of medicine and science where needs
Are met; building, religion, music, art,

History of food, dress, houses withal
To make people aware that we are part
Of a globe requiring knowledge of all.

The petty wars and battles in their place,
We must improve, uplift the human race.

HITCH-HIKING TO WORMWOOD SCRUBS

A beautiful day on the Great West Road
And we were coming home, three thumbing lifts

To London; so to avoid sudden rifts
I went on ahead with a lightweight load
On my shoulder. Cars, vans, lorries all passed
By but I walked on, happy in the sun,

Believing very soon a kind someone
Would stop and take me aboard. Then at last

A Green Line coach pulled up, a prison guard
Beckoned me in; I sat in the front seat.
Behind me, handcuffed to the rails, were eight
Convicts bound for Wormwood Scrubs with four, hard-

Faced warders as escort. At a cafe
One bought me tea and cake that summer day.

HOLY LAND

When I renew each day and dwell again
On matters which concern our planet, Earth,
I lament the desecration that men
Inflict on holy land, decry the dearth
Of love, joy and worship of Nature's art:
Its flowers, trees, lakes and brimming rivers
That take silent waters down to the heart
Of the sea. Could we not become givers
Of life and not destroyers in our time
Upon the land; each step we take is by
Consent of our Maker. If we, sublime
Souls that we are, put Earth in jeopardy,
Then we shall be self-punished for taking
An unwise life-course of our own making.

HOW TO SELL ICE CREAM

We sold ice cream once, my brother and I.

We had to earn money to help to pay
For studies, so worked for Mr Rossi

At Folkestone. We left the restaurant each day
On big, three-wheeled, ice-cream carts which we rode
Through the town to a designated site

On the cliff top by Harvey's statue, load
Of ice-cream on board and fan-sprays of light
Cones in their box for the public to see.
Early summer ... and we had to create

A market, stir up demand for icy
Cornets. Trade was slow ... commission not great
Till we ate things ourselves in public view,
Then people came and ate the cornets too.

HUMOUR IN A SONNET

Would you look for humour in a sonnet?
It is a solemn form, scholarly, grave
As mistress' eyebrow, dark as a bonnet
Worn at a funeral, and still a slave
To tradition – Milton, Shakespeare, Petrarch.
But time moves on and custom don't stand still.
Shall we loose the rein and ride in the park
In Rotten Row or canter up the hill

Of amusement? Shall we let light of eye
Twinkle as we go riding on for rhyme?
Dare we let the mare, or Muse, gallop high
Until we're out of step with former time?
Purists will forgive seeming levity
And thank the Lord for sonnet's brevity!

IN MY FATHER'S HOUSE

"In my Father's house are many mansions,"
Jesus said. Was He thinking of the sky
At night when he spoke? Stellar expansions
And their movements, known in astronomy
Today, perhaps were not known, then. Maybe
Jesus knew the constellations, their parts
And constituents and in speech made free
Use of them in His imagery, arts
That were His second nature. Reference
To the Great Universe, its mysteries,
Was appropriate, homely. Deference
Would be paid to the Son for centuries
To come; Christians uplifted, transported ...
In many mansions they'd be comforted.

IN PRAISE OF WOMEN

Rock against whom the wave of childhood breaks
In tearful onslaughts of uncertainty,
Demanding sun and moon like one who takes
Refusal as affront to dignity;
Crying, using emotion as a rod
To sway the mother willing to relent
And yield to the little one like a god
Who forgives the sinner and its intent.
These women who lull the cradles of men,
Who guide them through the pains of childhood's life
With never-ending love, are the fountains
Of the world, giving and dispensing, when
In the triple role of companion, wife
And mother they are steadfast as mountains.

INSECTS AND MAN

A small, black insect, not a mosquito,
Was biting my calf, drinking my life's blood.
I slapped him briskly before he could go

Away, but the damage was done: one good
Leg was infected; it began to itch
And by morning the infection had spread

Down the limb, accompanied by pain which
Increased when I got up off the bed.
How I cursed the insect world, the trouble

They cause to Man: mosquitoes, wasps and flies,
Ants, gnats, spiders, cockroaches that double
Their numbers over night; the moth that tries

Our patience at the light; even the bee
That dares to interrupt the ladies' tea.

IN THE BEGINNING WAS THE WORD

I think it is possible to deduce
The first word ever uttered, I won't say
Spoken, by earliest man. Not 'war', 'truce',
'Ultramarine' or anything deep, fey

Or abstract, just a short sound that became
The basis of language. Did a small child

Make a noise like 'da ... da'? Or a human
Female cry out in pain in a harsh, wild
Birth? Perhaps the first, primitive, male brute
Put his bare foot on a thorn and said, 'Damn!'

Other prime words could have been, 'ugh!' 'tree', 'fruit',
'Help!', 'kill!' ('me Tarzan, you Jane!') even 'scram!'

Whatever it was, first word takes the prize
For the birth of language – and deities!

IRISH LABOURERS – 1

These kindly men, these gentle, kindly men,
Helped me one summer when I went to work

On the site. Elderly, they did not shirk
Labouring but kept steadily on when
The noon sun was hot in the sky. They showed
Me how to shovel dirt, nudge with the knee

To help the arms, a little scoop and be
Leisurely, "Or you'll not last, me bhoy!" Road-

Clearing, rubble-digging, heaving cement,
Unloading a lorry full of bricks, five
Thousand from London brought in a late drive
As we were heading home. The driver meant

Well, so the men agreed to shift the load,
And two by two we stacked them by the road.

IRISH LABOURERS – 2

They could not read, these working Irishmen,
But they were kind and thoughtful of their kin:
Their brogue was lilting, mellow, do you ken,

And tough and strong they toiled through thick and thin.
And when the trolley brought the morning tea
We bought our mugs and Chelsea buns to eat,

To rest awhile, all drinking leisurely,
We found a hut to shelter from the heat.
The foreman had a paper in his hand

From which he read the news aloud each day;
He'd pause and wait, survey his little band,
And listen while the scholars had their say.

Then nourished by the news and tea and bun,
Resuming work we laboured in the sun.

ITALIAN WEDDING
3rd January 1999

The wedding was held in the cathedral
In Pescara, English, Italian guests
Assembled to witness the priest's twice-blessed
Marriage in two languages that would fall
With such harmony in that lovely place.
His people one side, hers on the other,
Uncles and aunts, her father and mother,
Warm-hearted, charming folk who came to grace

The occasion and give us all their love.
In the city we met that special day,
Wife in her role to give my son away ...
Boy become man, the man that I approve;

Simona, dear and beautiful before,
Was now his wife and a daughter-in-law.

ITCH!

Good God! How I itch! Some wretched insect
Has bitten my exposed, pink flesh and left
His venom in me as if he'd inject
Me purposely to make me mad. Bereft

Of all other senses, this one, small spot,
A bite that I can hardly see, pervades
All feeling, draws me to it and I've got
To scratch! This invisible mite invades

My being, attacks this human temple,
Inflicts pain and leaves me irritable.
Is there some way I could raise a pimple
On him and give him inevitable

Itching? Come winter and the blessed cold
When insects are all frozen, dead or old!

I'VE SPOKEN TO TWENTY PEOPLE TODAY

I've spoken to twenty people today,
Monday, second of July, weather fine:
Wife, plumber, a builder, Ruth, Caroline
And Ken, Carol, a new member to say

Welcome, Hugh, a solicitor, his wife,
Brenda, a sculptress, Helene who does
Catering, George, bowls player who has
Been active most of his natural life,

Theresa, Andy, Phil, the tennis coach,
Martin, his brother, Gina, a beauty
Specialist, two officials on duty
At the post office, both of whom could broach

A smile when I went in, and two old dears
With whom I strolled uphill: – best day for years.

JENNY STRUCK BY LIGHTNING

Jen was in the house when the lightning struck!
A maelstrom storm, wind and dark rain lashing
The street in anger, heavy clouds clashing

In fury overhead ... and Jenny's luck
Ran out. A bolt of blue lightning cut through
The house, a phantom of light invading

Her room, ethereally pervading
The air and passing her by as it blew
The telephone from the wall. Every light

Was affected, her TV, the fridge, all
Electrical appliances blown. Pall
Of darkness fell indoors like tempest night

Outside and Jenny thanked her guiding star
That she'd been spared the worst of Heaven's war.

JEPSON'S GRAMMAR

Of English grammar Jepson is the King:
His book, an *English Grammar For Today*,
Is designed to teach the young how they may
Use language, a medium for thinking
And speaking clearly. Seven parts of speech
Defined, not eight; interjections are passed
By and all seven subsequently cast
In one sentence for the student to teach
Him thus: 'My landlady always gives me
Bacon and eggs for breakfast.' Noun and verb,
Adjective, conjunction, pronoun, adverb,
Preposition, not in order, to be
Remembered. What a book to tease the mind!
And I would praise all other of its kind.

JOE'S HOT EAR

Young Joe, seven years old, brought up in Spain,
Had earache and complained to grandmother
That it hurt and also he had pain
In the side of his head. She had other
Duties in the house but quickly prepared

The traditional, peasants' remedy:
A cone of wrapped paper with the end flared,

Point inserted in the ear, end to be
Lit. The heat and smoke would go down the cone

To melt the wax and halt the infection ...
But a neighbour called ... before she was done
Joe's ear was on fire without protection.
"And what about your earache, Joe?" I said.
"Oh, that was cured but I had burns instead."

JOKER AT TENNIS

We had a joker at the club, a man
Whose idea of tennis was to make fun,

To laugh the while, and gurgle when he ran
To the net, soon as the game had begun.

He voiced pert remarks often and again,
Believing that his wit raised him above
The rest, and I was one of many men
Who disliked to be there. Even in love

Games he would grimace, jig and be jolly
To distract an opponent waiting to serve,
And once I thought to punish his folly
With a forehand drive which he would deserve.

He leered, crouched and jeered, still acting the goat,
Missed my fierce shot and took it in the throat!

KAHOUTEK

When comets pass and debris from the tail
Shoots into the atmosphere, to be seen
As an aerial display, a night scene
Of meteoric particles like hail
Cascading to earth in summertime's pale
Pretence of warmth and pleasure, then our green
Minds assume that God's handiwork has been
Revealed, as mystic as the Holy Grail;
But in the cold and sullen depths of space,
Where rock of ages orbits its own star
In endless cycles of motion, what share
Of His power is given to this place?
Do men understand? Matter from afar
Cannot provide the answer to our prayer.

KINGSGATE AVENUE

Road without turning, road of my dreaming,
Long, strong and straight in its slope to the sea ...
Gently descending, seems never-ending,

Carries me down to the place where I'd be.
Green as a meadow, verdant in passing,
Broad in conception its verges extolled,

Tree-lined, bewooded, shrubs in abundance,
Houses with gables and gardens of old.
Hotels with terraces, gateposts, driveways,

Houses of comfort when evening light glows,
Many of which sleep in their shrubbery,
Beautiful Kingsgate as everyone knows.
Avenue's riches are dear as a song ...
There in my mind is the place I belong.

KINGSGATE WALK

"Pork ... There's a subject!" Mr Pumblechook
Would cast about for a theme for his talk,
As I cast my eyes on a Kingsgate walk
Over a farmer's muddy field and took

In a plantation of cauliflowers,
Green, upgrowing, sturdy of leaf and stalk,
Thicker than trees in a wood, had to baulk
At counting their magnificent bowers.

Row upon row they ran to the skyline,
Vast armies of brave fellows all in green,
Disciplined, tall, upright in root and stem

As though on the march to conquer in time
All those opposing. God, they did not seem
Hostile but strong. Their peace would become them.

KUALA LUMPUR

Suffering from mosquito bites I lay
In the army hospital in K. L.

Awaiting the next treatment. Day by day
The brown scabs were broken with tweezers well

Into the wounds until the blood flowed free
Down both arms and legs, and then gentian
Violet was daubed in melancholy

Attempts to heal the flesh. Little mention
Of the pain I felt, Doctor! These damn sores
Were as round as shillings on all my limbs

And red blood mingled with bright purple scores
Until I was bound again with lint trims

And bandages. On the bed I lay prone,
Wrapped like half a mummy bled to the bone.

N.B. K. L. – Kuala Lumpur, Malaya

LEARNING LATIN

I do admire linguists, those who can speak
In other tongues. We learned some French at school

And used to labour over the verbs week
By week, but among scholars we would fool
No one. Later I thought I'd learn Latin,

Bought a book to teach myself and began
With nouns, declensions and cases, sat in
My room late at night until eyelids ran
Down like shutters for sleep. I had trouble

With genders, no logic or reason there:
'*Nûbês*', a cloud, masculine – the bubble
Burst; all the clouds I had ever seen were

Feminine: soft, rounded, fluffy and white ...
I gave up Latin, read English at night.

LET'S EXAMINE THE VIRTUES

Let's examine the virtues, make a list
Of those that become a man and let him
Study it, in Bacon's words weigh the gist
And ponder how he might, at his own whim,
Find improvement. Courage and honesty
In dealings with his peers – can they have trust
In his judgement and mark him down wholly
Man: kind, tolerant, forgiving? We must
Forgive those who do not know what they do.
Generous and patient – Ah, yes, this last
Virtue is a godsend to all those who,
Like Milton, stand and wait, for in the past
Men served their God; but now, friend and brother,
Let us make haste and serve one another.

LIFE ON EARTH

Our dear Earth teems with life in all its forms:
Fish, beetles, bugs and reptiles, gnats, small birds ...
Thousands of species seem to be the norm,
Land and sea crammed with life; there are not words

Enough to emphasise how much: flatworms,
Roundworms, molluscs, snails, bivalves, shrimps and dabs,

All creatures fleet of foot and pachyderms,
Things of the air: all butterflies and crabs ...
And people by the million breathing air ...
All, all, parented by the sun above

Which lights the space about us everywhere
And generates the life we know and love.

A million suns still burning in the sky
Creating life throughout the galaxy.

LIGHTHOUSE

Tall upon the green headland, straight and white,
The lighthouse stands, a beacon at its crest.
Since fourteen ninety-nine at dark it sent
Its cliff-top warning to all ships at sea,

To mariners of old scanning at night
The harsh lines of shore when the sun sank west,
And cheered by its kindly welcome glow bent
Canvas north, south, in waters straight and free.

In early times how they laboured to light
The ship's course with lantern, oil lamp or best
Coal by the ton as fire to the urgent
Sky to keep loved ones safe from jeopardy!

Now electric, automatic, it shines
Twenty miles to sea when the day declines.

LIGHT OF HEAVEN

How happy people are when in the sun!
Their Father smiles on them and they smile back;
Like children they respond and off they run,
To dance and play in sunlight that they lack.
In his gold rays folk saunter out of doors
To sport in park or field or coastal beach;
Their gaiety in summer none deplores,
Their holiday is like the fruited peach.

These islands, dark and cloudy in the year,
A harbour to its peoples so oppressed,
Respond with life and laughter when the dear
Sire of Heaven returns and rules his best.
A shaft of sunlight brings an August smile
And Father winks and closes eyes awhile.

LONELINESS

There are so many women in the town
Who live alone in houses or in rooms;
Their solitude a weight to bear them down,
To shackle them in greyness or in glooms.
A husband has relinquished mortal life,

To leave a widow fending for herself;
She sallies forth as bravely as a wife,
As lonely as a woman on the shelf.
It is a tragic thing to hear their loss,
Their menfolk gone, to leave their hearts in tears,

And life's last, lonely banquet is a cross
That they will have to bear for years and years.
What strength they have, these women in dark rooms
Who live alone; no love their life illumes.

LONGING FOR AUTUMN

The weather's too hot ... this unremitting
Sunshine that from a clear, cerulean
Sky scorches this isle with Herculean
Heat is too much for me. As for sitting

Or lying on the blaze-bright beach the while,
That is not an indulgence I adore;
An Anglo-Saxon skin does not care for
Burning any more than toast. A roof tile

Bakes above, but not my poor flesh which needs
Cool breezes and colder, autumnal airs
To help it breathe. Winter's bracing cold bears
No ill will to Northerners, it brings seeds

Of Spring's fresh crispness, morning and at eve,
And that's comfort when frost is on the sleeve.

LOSS OF TRUST

She told me a sad tale in later years:
A child at home, some three to four in age;
Tea with her parents and no hint of tears
To come, nor could she small and young presage

Unhappiness that day. For Sunday treat
A promised meal: custard trifle and cake,
Her own teddy-bear plate, knife, fork, spoon meet
For her to own, small possessions to make

Her feel secure. And toying with her food,
As children do, she kept the cherry last,
In imagination reward for good
Behaviour – her father ate it! Aghast

At what the gruff, appalling man had done –
"That will teach you not to trust anyone!"

LUCY AND THE BIG BRAIN

Anthropologists tell us that this Earth
Was once the Planet of the Apes. Some eight
Million years ago their race topped the tree
Of evolution and the origin
Of Man was a mystery. Then the skull
Of the elusive ape in Africa

Was found: 1470, six hundred
Cc's in size. Then came Lucy: her small
Pelvis meant she was bipedal. Was Big-
Brain Ape or Lucy the real ancestor
Of Man? But 1470 was twice
Lucy's brain and man's origin in doubt.

Later, the skull of Flat-Faced Man appeared ...
Is Homo sapiens now emerging?

MAJESTY OF SPACE

Empty now the long, amber beach runs straight
Between rampart cliffs and the moated sea,
Scoured new by the ebbing tide, its state

Washed clean and passing dry. Firm and easy
Underfoot we can walk afar or stand
Among the white sea-shells and debris left

On the shore, great vistas at our command.
Ships sleep on the ocean, sea-birds so deft
In flight skim the shallows by silver shores,
Shearwaters, black and white, in their small droves

Wheel above the leaden waves, turn before
Our eyes and turn again. The scene behoves

Our homage to the majesty of space,
Earth, sea and sky and sea-birds with their grace.

MARITIME SPRING CLEAN

The season is upon us once again,
The yacht is trestled, waiting on the quay;
Her hull is tarnished with the winter rain,
Green-blighted with the algae from the sea.
Six months she's lain upon the sandy shore,
Her lashings on and resting in her stocks,
Sharp prow aligned to seaward, ever more
Eager for spring, the launch and summer clocks.
We scrub the deck and air Bermuda sails,
And paint her clinkers Oxford blue and white,
Then oil the clips and runners in their trails
And run the halyards up the masted height.
When *Jenny's* trim and set to show her pace
We launch and sail close-hauled to win the race!

MIND AND MATTER

Men have taught that Mind seated in the brain
Is special to Man, a great faculty
Which lifts him above all other creatures
And sets him apart from dross and matter.
The Mind of Man with its capacity
For thought is the absolute pinnacle
Of Creation, for with his Mind he could
Comprehend his Maker; but Winwood Reade
In his dynamic work, *The Martyrdom*
Of Man, wrote that 'Mind is a property
Of matter; matter is inhabited
By Mind'. Is it conceivable that Mind
Permeates the living and non-living?
That Intelligence is housed in the stars?

MISS PERKINS

When the day came our masters went to war,
The school was closed, the older men contrived
To give lessons and we, the pupils, were

Part-time. On Tuesday noon when we arrived
For two hours, sirens sounded and raids
Often sent us to shelter underground.

That meant lessons gone, we could not parade
Our learning – there was none. Then to astound
Us Miss Perkins came; she kept us in awe:

A fresh, midsummer night's dream who taught art;
We had not seen this Helena before
And we loved her with all our boyish heart.

Miss Perkins in view and we were in thrall ...
Problem with discipline? No, none at all!

MONSIEUR ALEXIS SOYER

At his own expense Monsieur Alexis
Soyer, famous chef of the Reform Club,
Journeyed to Scutari to assist Miss

Nightingale at the hospital. A tub
Of meat for the wounded, cut, boiled and dished
Unfairly, gave some all bone. A stupid

Regulation this and men were nourished
Ill. Soyer built ovens, baked biscuits, bread,

Prepared tureens of thick soup for the men
Neglected by the authorities till
Miss Nightingale arrived. Alexis then
Made a teapot for fifty which he'd fill

And keep hot. It's no wonder the lads cheered
When Alexis came, a chef they revered.

MORNING NEWSPAPER

I love *The Daily Telegraph* to read
Each morning; it helps to wake the sleeper
From rest. The first hot drink, milked and sugared,
Nectar to the thirsty mind, gives deeper

Pleasure till quenched then international
News follows: what's happening in Iraq
Where Saddam is making emotional
Gestures for his regime? Israel gives back
Land to Palestine but Intifada
Continues, for these people will not love
Their neighbour as themselves, so it's harder
To bring peace to those who put hate above

All else. And if this does not clear my head
And wake me up, then back I go to bed!

MOSQUITOES

He had returned from holiday in Crete
Where he had savoured sunshine, beach and sea,
A rugged island, old in history,
The birthplace of Zeus, the Lord, no mean feat
Since he was the God of Gods. But ancient
Lore, classic skies, mountains and sunlit tracks
Were marred by death's mosquitoes at their backs
Plaguing white-skinned visitors with penchant

For their blood. Where in Zeus's scheme of things
Do these deft vampires, these blood-drinking mites
Fit, since their detested, malignant bites
Cause death, havoc to all men and to Kings?

With him I curse these instruments of fate
And pray that Science can obliterate.

MOTHER AND HER EELS – 1

When I was a boy Mother would take me
To the market in London to buy fish
From a barrow boy's stall. "All fresh, lady!
Straight from the sea! They swam here just to wish
You luck. Now, what'll you have?" On display

From Billingsgate were herring, plaice and skate,
Mackerel, kippers, dabs and an array
Of shellfish that would tempt any man's plate:
Cockles and mussels, prawns, oysters, crabs, shrimps,
Winkles in black shells – "'Ere, you got a pin?"

And when you do buy the barrow boy skimps
Nothing, good for trade that keeps coming in.

But Mother's speciality, Dad feels
The same, writhing in their metal crate – eels!

MOTHER AND HER EELS – 2

At the barrow in the market Mother
Would deliberate, looking, as she knows
How, at the day's fish for sale: "No bother,
Love. You take yer time – Roes! Fresh herring roes!
Pair o'kippers, cheap!" Then she'd make her move:

Two large skate, two plaice, cockles, shrimps, winkles ...
The barrow boy would beam and say, "Right, love,
Right, love!" and wait again while she wrinkles
Her nose and points, "And half a dozen eels."
These eels are live, black, slithey things. He wraps

Them up, puts them in her bag and looks, feels
Pleased with custom. As we go home a chap

Calls, "Hey, Missus! An eel's escaped!" No feet,
It's free and wriggling off up the street!

MOTHER AND HER EELS – 3

Mother didn't hesitate, she gave chase;
One of her precious eels running away?
An eel that she had paid for? Its high place
On the supper table, chopped, cooked same day,
Served in a creamy, parsley sauce for Dad

After work, add vinegar and pepper,
A dish of bread and best butter; how glad
The appetite for sweet, soft flesh. Kippers
Are brown, of course; eel flesh is purest white.
Mother left me with the shopping bag, ran

Up the street and caught her live eel, delight
Visible to all, wrapped him up again

And marched us home. Live eels are very fine ...
She chopped him first, first in the firing line!

MR BAIRD

Five fifteen in the morning Mr Baird
Opens the shop, carries in the thick stacks

Of papers, lights the gas radiators
To warm the place, smokes and briskly attacks
The day's newsprint: *Mirror, Herald* and *Mail,*

Express, Chronicle, Telegraph, Times, black
Pencil scalloping big numbers on top
Of each from his dog-eared, rounds book, and back
And forth his hands circle in smooth motion,

Grey smoke drifts, spirals from cheerful lips while
He works. He greets his boys as they stumble
In from the dark, cold streets, their morning pile
Of papers set for them to deliver.
"Warm yourselves, boys," he says when they shiver.

MR BECKER

Dressed like the Aga Khan in a neat, dark-
Grey, pinhead suit from West End's Savile Row,
And a cream, silk shirt with long cuffs that go
Well with his hands; a blue, gold-stripe tie, mark

Of college days, he has a distinction
He carries well; a fine head, a deep brow,
Firm, strong jaw and clear, ice-blue eyes that bow
To no one, stamp him as a gentleman

At least and perhaps an aristocrat.
He walks through the Room at Lloyds like a lord
Among men seeking mutual accord
With underwriters, mind on the market,

A marine broker: ships await his beat
To sail the seas when business is complete.

MR BRAMBLE

The cashier to the firm, Mr Bramble,
  Habitually sour-faced and grim,

Brought the wages on Friday. He'd amble
  In with his bad leg, tall, stooping and slim
  As a hook and appear like a sere, grey
Ghost with his tray of brown packets small-stacked

In rows, his hawkish hand hiding the pay
  We were to receive. We thought that he lacked

Humanity. "Put that in your pocket,
  My boy!" he'd whisper, as though wages were
  A foul thing to be concealed. No docket
Inside – one pound, twelve and six. You'd infer

We were underpaid: the truth you detect.
  We bore him no love, not even respect.

MR CHAIRMAN

Do not give up your seat, Mr Chairman,
Do not resign; two full years in office

Have been marked with distinction which no one
Could have exceeded. No one will suffice
In your place. It is not of your making
That conflict has arisen, that members

Have complained of conduct unbecoming
In Captains of teams and that embers

Of discord have been raked anew this year.
Let those who cause a stir be themselves stirred!
Let it be known to them that their unfair
Line needs to be corrected. Be assured

That Chairmen outrank Captains in the show;
Stand fast! It is the lesser men who go.

MR CLINK

Pink-complexioned, round-faced, small, rich and fat,
A pudding on short legs, wrapped in a suit
Of expensive cloth, with a pink shirt that
Matched chubby cheeks, Mr Clink was a brute

To inferiors who came to his door.
Often abroad on business or living
At The Savoy, Managing Director
Of a City broking firm and giving
Offence where none was due, he would snap, shout
At the Managers and Brokers each day.

As office boy I loved to get about
With letters and, summoned, I heard him say,
"Son, I want you to do a little job;
Take my case to the hotel — here's five bob!"

MR GILBERT REFUSES – 1

I'd paid for the lessons and wrote for a test,
Withdrew half my savings and purchased a car;
A jaunt to the office to make a request
For absence from teaching the curricula.

To stern Mr Gilbert I entered my pleas,
An afternoon's freedom, three hours at most:
"I've taken tuition, a car would soon ease
The day trip to Sandwich along the east coast.

"A colleague could cover me for a brief spell."
But stern Mr Gilbert was grim – he refused,
And leaving his presence, determined as well,
I have to admit I was cross and confused.
I took my first test and I failed, sad to say,
And kind Mr Gilbert withheld a day's pay.

MR GILBERT REFUSES – 2

A teacher's nine-year son at Repton School
Was due to journey home in mid July;
In letters to his mother he made full
Pleas to be met at the halt station by
The crossing. Mrs T. was at her best

In biology; girls were keen to pass.
The lady saw the Head and her request –
A colleague to relieve her in her class.
The man refused! She argued for her son,
"The station's not a station, it's remote!"

And for his sake absconded when she'd done,
To bring him home, his luggage and his coat.
Next day she penned a letter to resign,
Became a Head – a better Head than mine.

MR SMITH BOWLING

One of the joys of this life was to watch
Mr Smith bowling. In the yearly match

Against the boys he would captain the staff
On the field of play and bowl to boys half

His height and stagger them with his odd style.
A slow lobber over the wicket while

The boys wondered how the Old Man would play,
He'd trot to the crease in his portly way,

Red cricket cap tucked in his belt, and throw
The leather up in a great, curving bow

Of tormenting flight, hit the pitch and stop ...
The boy would swing hard and fall neck and crop.

Mr Smith would take any lad's wicket
Who couldn't play unreachable cricket.

MRS VAN DEN BERG

A quarter to five, the telephone rings
On her desk and she snaps at the late call:

"Come in, Mrs V., will you, and do bring
Your notebook," says the Manager with all
Courtesy and at once Mrs V. flaps.
Her desk is a heap of paper – letters,

Cover notes, policies, slips and perhaps
She'll find her shorthand notebook. She'd better

Hurry; she stirs the heap with hot, red hands,
Finds her old notebook, needs a pencil now
And can't find one; searches a drawer ... "The man's
A menace!" through tight teeth. She finds a brown

Stub and lurches to the door while he waits;
Her shorthand's not the best when he dictates.

MR WOOD DINES

I can remember Woodie having lunch
At school, sandy-haired, flush-faced, not too tall;
We would collect our meal from the server
And, as staff, sit up on stage in the hall

To dine. At once Woodie would take up knife
And fork and begin at speed, no delay;
In large amounts the hot food was transferred
From plate to mouth and swallowed in a way

That was astonishing: he did not chew
Or seem to need teeth; a snatch and a fast
Dispatch of mash, greens and minced beef from dish
To stomach before I'd napkined and passed

The salt. In a minute or two, I guess,
He had finished as I peppered the cress.

MR WOOD IN THE GARDEN

Woodie was gardening that afternoon,
Taking for their lesson a lower-stream
Group, big, slow-witted lads who'd very soon
Want a change of occupation, day-dream
Boys who were not averse to derision,
Fun or games if they could slyly do so.

Woodie was sharp on his supervision
And dealt instant justice to lads who'd throw
Stones or lumps of earth and in noon-day heat
He saw a boy who erred and rebuked him.

"Ya - Ya!" the youth cried at the master – feet
Left the hot ground as Old Woodie floored him!
"Serves him right!" they said as the youth got up;
"Shouldn't be rude – Cor! sir's got a wallop!"

MUDFLAPS

Mudflaps do not make an elevated
Theme for a sonnet; they are the lowly
Appendages of a car which slowly
Clog with grime and appear devastated
With wheel-spin dust and mishaps from the road.
Hung between the low body and the wheel
They are like old men's shoes worn down at heel,
Weathered, damp, rugged, even slightly bowed.

Where is their glory, their considered note
Of praise? They do not rank with the plushy
Parts of elegant interiors, lace
Curtains, polished wood or perhaps the haute
Couture of wives who do not like mushy
Things which keep the dirt in its unseen place.

MUSIC OF THE GODS

What would life be without the godly sound
Of music? Violin and piano
Concertos, opera, symphonies so

Beautifully played by orchestras round
The world? Mendelssohn and Rachmaninov,
Puccini; four, five and six, Tchaikovsky,

And *Boris Godunov* by Mussorgsky,
Marches by Elgar, Rimsky-Korsakov's
Scheherazade, *Porgy and Bess*, Gershwin;

Symphonies and the *Karelia Suite*
Of Finland's Sibelius, the complete
Ninth of Dvořák, *Prince Igor*, Borodin.

These pieces, and more, which I will never
Forget, I could hear again for ever.

MYSTERY OF THE HUMAN BODY

It breathes, moves and functions in all its parts,
Hands co-ordinated, fraternal twins,
Progeny of the brain, fuelled by heart

And lungs, love's powerhouse and dear engine
Of the body. Bipedal on its limbs,
It carries intelligence across land

Masses, a lithe, working miracle, trim,
Wrought, unified, organised as though planned,
Devised and built to specification.

The mouth, a mother with its gifts of speech,
Eating, drinking, kissing, breathing action,
One small base supporting the role of each

Function. Do we not marvel at its fate
And thank the Grand Designer of our state?

MY TOOTHBRUSH

I would not be parted from my toothbrush!
It is, they are, my loyal, faithful friends.
In fact, I have half a dozen I blush
To admit, all sorts, all colours, on ends
In a green beaker on the window ledge
In the bathroom, and I use them three, four
Times a day. Also 'Interdens', a wedge
Of thin wood for gaps between the teeth. More
Than this is a blue, bottle brush that probes
To the back of a molar and removes
Debris the others cannot reach. It robes
Them in white and freshness. I would our loves
Could all be honey, sweeter in the breath –
A toothbrush is the thing that I'd bequeath!

NARROW BOAT

Give me a holiday on a narrow boat
On the canals of England. Let me float

In shallow, still waters at a fast speed
Of four miles an hour, cruising by the reeds

That fret the banks. What luxury aboard
The vessel which is not too wide or broad

In the beam but compensates in its length,
Forty-five feet of splendid timber, strength

In the bow, sides, decking, and an engine
To drive her, marine diesel, that has been

Faultless for a week! The central heating
Provides hot water for showers, beating

Chill nights on the river ... and there's no haste
For tranquil men who have no time to waste.

NATURAL DISASTERS

The planet jars and trembles when its plates
Tectonic seethe and grind; huge forces rise
To shatter the crust, to crush urban states
And raze village dwellings with their surprise
Shocks: Turkey, Iran, India, the Far

East, Japan, subject to the cruel schemes
Of Nature which bring terror to all bar
None. Mount Etna spews hot magma which steams
And, running red, destroys all life below.
Tornadoes in America rampage

Across the dry plains and hurricanes blow
In Miami, Florida, all in rage
Along the coast. What hope do puny men
Have when Nature's disasters strike again?

NATURE'S FIRST COURSE

My brother insists that he does not sleep
Soundly as he would wish. He wakes at night,
Yearns to embrace an embalmed slumber, deep
And restful, but denied solace recites
Poetry instead of counting the sheep
Of harvest time: 'The curfew tolls the knell ...'
And, 'For men must work and women must weep ...'
'When Sam goes back in memory ...' on well
Into the small hours. Would a PhD
Occupy his mind, make him feel weary,
Instead of daily swimming in the sea
Which does not render eyes red and bleary?
Shakespeare got it wrong; I'm sure to endorse
That for man sleep is 'great Nature's *first* course.'

NIGHT WORK

Now I must lay me down and go to sleep,
For weariness has dulled my aching brain,
And lulled by warmth, stillness, no light to keep
Awake, I'll slumber till I rise again.
Once renewed, fed, watered, I'll take my pen
And labour at the sonnet I must write,
Knowing that the task will be fulfilled when
My seething Muse is clearer in the light.
This task of love, resumed when I'm awake,
Goes on at night if I'm disturbed from rest,
And hoping to complete the work I take
Up the day-slack and pencil in at best.
A final couplet and the poem's done,
I douse the light and smile, and slumber on.

OLD BILL'S REPORTS

The term was coming to an end at school:
Examinations and summer reports
To be written with grades, comments in full,
Including PE and relevant sports.

Old Bill, rustic Toby-jug in brown, tweed
Coat, taught Natural History sessions
In the garden with boys who would clear weeds,
Dig, plant and grow crops. At his discretion

They would work in the classroom. The reports
Came to Bill, fifteen boys and fifteen girls
Per class, and leisurely with little snorts
Of pleasure, he wrote with old-fashioned twirls:

'Good in the garden!' for dainty Miss Benn
And her friends. Oh dear! We did them again.

OLD THINGS

I have a love of old things, not the new,
Old clothes, old shoes, old houses, churches, too;
I have a jacket, lightweight, which I bought
Twenty-five years ago and so I ought,
By decent standards of dress to discard,
And yet, like a dear old friend, it is hard

To throw away; I love its friendly arms,
Its old-world, old, olive-green feel, its charms;

It embraces my shoulders, faithful friend,
It gives me warmth, comfort and has no bend
In its soft fabric – zip sound, the cuffs frayed,
The pockets holed, the lining split and splayed ...
It's nearly past its best, it ought to go ...
Yet it is true to me – I love it so.

OLD WHISTLER

My daughter came and burnt the kettle dry!

It had a dead whistle which did not sing,
But we were in the habit of watching

'Old Whistler' closely till it boiled, so why
Not do the same, daughter dear? But busy
With children of her own she had to deal

With bottoms and a napkin and the tea
Was forgotten while she saw to the real
Business of childhood. All the water went
Up in steam, Whistler's bottom grew red-hot,

The plastic handle melted as it got
Burnt and very soon small, black bits were sent
Aloft like soot. Ah! The smell! Then a cough!
She ran to the stove, turned Old Whistler off.

ONE STUMP

We used to practise bowling at one stump,
Ted and I. We would go down to the park
With our gear, a cricket ball and *one stump*,

Pace out twenty-two yards and bowl till dark,
A coat at one end, stump at the other;
Ted would bowl six and I would keep wicket

With bare hands and then we would change over;
My turn to bowl to improve our cricket.
We had reasoned thus as young, sporting chaps:

At Lord's they practise in the nets with three
Stumps to aim at; we have one and perhaps
We shall be more accurate – we shall see.

'Anyone can hit the lot!' we had said;
My Dad could at seventy, bless his head.

ONE-WAY STREET

We went into town to collect a book.
Returning, we left the main road and took
A short-cut through a quiet, narrow street.
Ahead, a white van, parked, two cars and feet
To spare. No room to pass. The route was blocked.
I waited, engine idling, and soon clocked
The time. Nothing moved, so I thought – 'Reverse!'
Reluctant to sit there doodling, averse
To wasting time, and swung the car to make
A neat two-point turn. An old loon, awake
Of a sudden, becapped, arm raised, quick cried,
"This is a one-way street!" – "Shut up!" I sighed
After my outburst, shook my heated head;
Until that moment loon was almost dead.

OPERATION ROSEBUD – 1

My Helen took her daughter, Jess, in hand,
   To try to put some colour in her cheeks;
A bright child from birth, education planned,
   It had produced results; and a few weeks

After she was five Jessica could read
   Aloud from *The Oxford Book of English*
Verse: *The Listeners*, Walter de la Mare, heed
   What she was saying and distinguish

'Traveller, descended, phantom,' such words
   An older child would blink at; but scholar
Though she was, her cheeks were white when the birds
   Came to her window and sang while collar

Doves strutted on the lawn. Helen agreed
That 'Operation Rosebud' should proceed.

OPERATION ROSEBUD – 2

Long holidays were set to bring the child
To Broadstairs and the sea. Jess would become
An outdoor girl, play in the sun and mild
Winds the season brings, and walk, skip and run
Every day, morning and noon, exercise
Her limbs, fill inland lungs with pure sea air
That breasts in from the east. How she would prize
Sweet hours of mother's play upon the fair

Beach, deserted in the cool, late Spring when
Summer crowds have not yet begun. Legs, arms
Would be strong, her young breath deepen, and then
Her appetite would bloom, her dear face warm

To pinken cheeks like the July blush-rose
That we remember when the blossom goes.

PALI CANON

I did not enjoy the Pali Canon
Much as I had hoped. It seemed vague, diffuse,
Unworldly, a long concatenation
Of discourse and counter discourse, abstruse,
Not entirely steeped in Western logic,
So that I laboured through an intricate
Maze of metaphor so pedagogic
I had to read it again, extricate
A hidden thread and hold it to the light.
And four, basic elements: extension,
Cohesion, heat and motion are not right
For they defy simple comprehension.
I'll return the book to its Eastern shelf
Next 'Thou shalt love thy neighbour as thyself.'

PALINDROMES

My boy came home from school with news to tell
Of phrases on the board to write in class:
'Palindromes' he called them, remembered well,
I thought, and showed me two that would surpass
A simple phrase. First, 'Madam, I'm Adam,'
Clearly read from his own handwritten text,

Then, 'Rats live on no evil star,' a sad
Indictment of society, was next.

"I have to find words," he said, "that will read
Both ways from front and back." I thought of 'noon'

And 'level'; we drew a list that would need
No checking and, pen to paper, I soon
Drafted more: 'Nurses run!' his page to fill,
And then I wrote 'Lid Off A Daffodil.'

PEBBLES ON THE BEACH AT DEAL

I sat on the shore of a timeless sea,
On a vast beach of smooth-cornered pebbles,
Pondering how many, a quantity
Beyond counting like the trills and trebles
Of larks that ever sang. And then each day
Pebbles brown and cream, blue and grey would be
Unnumbered as stars in the Milky Way.
How smooth, pleasant to the touch, how firmly
They lie in patterned heaps forever still
Unless pounding waves, human foot or hand
Should disturb them or despoil their tranquil
Rest. These admirable gems of life, first land
Under Caesar's tread, know their valued place
As guardians of a doughty island race.

PIGEONS IN TRAFALGAR SQUARE

The new Mayor of London, dressed in red socks,
Wants to ban pigeons from Trafalgar Square.
He calls them vermin, says he cannot bear
Them – why not pull the plug on London Docks?

Or stop the fountains, close St Martin's Church?
Move Nelson's Column to another site?
Burn the National Gallery one dark night?
And leave a million tourists in the lurch.

Pigeons, move the pigeons, you foolish Mayor?
He will not license Tom who sells the seed
To visitors who love to pose and feed
Birds for photographs taken in the square.

Sooner than banish pigeons from their haunt,
Ban the Red Mayor, send him off to Gaunt.

PLAGUES OF PEOPLE

Too many people are born on the Earth,
Where vast crowds swarm in the world's great cities;
Two or three sit by the small, country hearth,

Sing to the child their immortal ditties.
The Blue Planet reels with myriad forms
Which are so aptly termed 'the human race'

And burgeoning numbers exceed the norms
Of those who endure in an urban place.
A nest of black ants, a swarm of brown bees,

A plague of locusts, wasps, hideous flies
Fill us with loathing and our hearts' unease
Yearns to find solace in pale blue skies.

A plague of people, a billion dead souls
Is not, I would think, one of Nature's goals.

POOR, POOR WOMAN

A poor, poor woman with a battered face
Appeared in the warm cafe late at night,
Sat in the seat opposite, had a fight,

I suppose, and stared at my full, hot plaice
And chips. Her swollen cheeks were brown and blue,
Her sad eyes bruised and black, her lips all puffed

With pain. She took a piece of fish and stuffed
Her mouth, ate a discarded chip or two
And looked for more. Embarrassed and quite stunned

By the woman's dumb plight, I have to say
I acted badly, not a Christian way;
I could have bought her a meal from my fund.

I had a boat to catch from Portsmouth Dock.
Her face still haunts me; its memory – shock!

PRE-DECIMAL CURRENCY

Six shillings and seven-pence three-farthings
It amounted to in a glass-topped case,
Pre-decimal currency set in rings

Of silk, coins sterling which had a warm place
In the hearts of people. Then to confound
In nineteen seventy-two conversion:

Two hundred and forty pence to the pound
To a hundred! What a dire subversion
Of wealth! Half-crown, florin, shilling, sixpence,

Threepence in silver and threepence in brass,
Penny, halfpenny, farthing, all dispensed
With, good, substantial coinage set to pass

Away from English hands and English hearts
To suit the way of life in other parts.

PRINCE ALBERT

Prince Albert, husband of Victoria,
Queen of England, had a reputation
For being mean – *sic transit gloria* ...
Ruthless to all those of lesser station
When money was concerned, he soon had charge
Of house affairs at Buckingham Palace

Where, to reduce expenses, he made large
Cuts in wages to housemaids. Young faces
Fell when their forty-five pounds for the year
Was reduced to twelve! Five shillings a week!

A retired labourer on his books, dear
Pensioned at a pound a month, had to seek
Parish support when Albert would not pay ...
Despicable meanness the Consort way!

QUANTUM THEORY AND VAN GOGH

Reading two things simultaneously
Is pabulum for the mind: first feature,
The life in a coloured biography

Of Vincent Van Gogh, linguist and teacher
In England, pastor in the Borinage
Where he gave his possessions to the poor;

Salesman for Goupil, but his persiflage
And truth threw his prospects out of the door.
As a strong contrast the next article

Deals with Quantum Theory, photons of light
That are wave motion or a particle
Of matter and either, or, is not right.

I prefer Van Gogh whose work I could buy;
Plank's Quantum is uncertain as the sky.

QUIZ

They asked us all the things I did not know,
   Not tapping in to half my store of wit;
   And so I sat, a dumb-bell at the show,

   A member of a team that relished it.
The quiz rolled on, we struggled hard to win:

Pop groups, TV duffs, songs I'd never heard,
   Cyclists, lady tennis champs of yore, gin
   Tonic drinks? Oh, ignorance is the word!

   I do not find a quiz a useful game,
   For knowledge is a semi-precious stone

And what we know is never quite the same
As other men's who make their wit their own.
   If I could ask the questions then I'd score:
   'And who was Mirza Yahya heretofore?'

RED TABLETS

A continuous ache in the right knee
Through playing too much soccer, cartilage
Trouble, no doubt, began to worry me
And I dreamt of crippling surgery which

Would end my long love of sport. A visit
To the doctor and told him of my pain,
But he did not flinch or take exquisite
Care to examine me; he wrote a plain
Prescription – "Good day!" I took fifty red
Tablets home, put the bottle on the shelf,
Looked severely at it, said to myself,
"How do they know the good leg from the bad"'

And declined to take the drug. No matter.
A few weeks' rest and my knee got better.

REFEREE

'Four with the hands, three with the feet and two
With the body.' These were the rules I had
To apply when I was a referee.
In soccer there are penal offences
For which a direct free kick is then due.
A blast on the whistle, point to the bad
Man who has kicked a player in the knee
And indicate the spot. Goalie tenses
On his line, shouts at his defenders who
Are not covering and sighs when the lad
Boots the ball over the bar. Glance to see
If the linesman has come to his senses
And let play go on. 'Ref, you've done enough ...
Keep yourself fit and don't run out of puff!'

REPOINTING THE CHIMNEY STACK

The company that advanced the mortgage
To buy the house wanted the chimney stack
Repointed. First quote: scaffold to the ridge,
Two hundred pounds. Second quote: from a Jack-
Of-all-trades with his ladders, one hundred
And thirty. I told Roy I would repoint

For him. We mixed cement which I carried
Up to the roof and secured each brick joint
That was loose, holding on to a guide rope
We had rigged round the stack to stop my fall.

While I was working on the steep, tiled slope
I reckoned the cost to my brother all
Round – he was in a monetary fix –
No charge for labour ... just thirteen and six!

ROWING ON THE LAKE

A small boat clinker-built of light, brown wood
Cresting on the flat waters of the lake
Is a shell of beauty. I love to take
Up oars and with infinite care, nor should
I disturb a perfect scene, ease the craft

Into motion, set oars and let them dip
As scarce to make a ripple. Rare wine sips
Slow; in long, rhythmic touches fore and aft
I pull gently away as one who lives
Well on lake water, then dip and pull, lift

And feather the blades like wood on glass, rift
And ripple soothing my heart. That which gives
Joy alone on the lake is to be well
Remembered, sweet sound of a distant bell.

ROY'S CRASH

While riding on a motorbike to school
One January morning, winter-white,
The fields were blue with frost, the bare trees full
Of rime and in the lane ahead, turn right,

The corner by the church in view. His books
Were in the sidecar swept by bitter cold,
And black above the steeple turn, the rooks
Started up in elm trees tall, made wing bold

By his approach to take the bend. A jar!
The wheel had locked! And while he wrenched again
The bike went through the churchyard fence – a bar
Had snapped, the side fell and the luckless man

Invaded sacred ground, stop-launched alone,
And later woke athwart an ancient stone.

RUNNING WITH NORMAN

We two ran together, Norman and I,
Representing the youth club. He was strong,
Deep-chested, muscular; our strategy

Was to run as a team, to string along
The opposition and make them respond
To our plan: he would sprint from the start gun

And take the field with him, the pace beyond
Their wish with Norman out in front. I'd run
Slowly at the rear till I got my breath,

Then I'd accelerate and overtake
The lot, Norman included. He at death's
Gasp would hold on with his strength and would make

A supreme effort to be second, third;
His was the credit, sacrifice deferred.

RUSTOM OPERATES

Invited to observe in theatre
I was given a gown to don, a mask,
A green, surgical cap and far better
Prepared for blood than I knew, I was passed
Into a brightly lit, clinical room
Where Rustom, an orthopaedic surgeon,
Was to operate on an old woman
To replace her hip. No hesitation.

A long incision in depth to expose
The joint, then saw, hammer, chisel, remove
The head of the femur, fit prosthesis
Into the bone, close, stitch with gut above –

I watched my friend in silence and in awe;
I'd never seen such brilliant work before.

RUSTOM'S MISSION

Go abroad, Rustom, and lie in the sun,
Absorb the heat that's missing in these isles,
Welcome the lucent days that seem to come
Unasked for, worshipped and soon met with smiles.
This land of ours has bred a rugged soul
Who views dark skies and winter greys with scorn,
Who's suffered rain, raw winds, snow and the whole
Gamut of bleak weather since he was born.
Go to Iberia, there rest each day
Until your blood is warm, your tendon healed;
Declare your mission, it's the only way
To promulgate a faith that's not concealed.
Bless your enterprise, my friend, ease your heart,
Return to us as soon as summers start.

SAILING OFF A LEE SHORE – 1

Small yachts brought to a sea-wind, brisk, lee shore,

Loose-foot jibs flying but the mains not free,
And the white waves pounding the beach soon bore

Sailors to land with the wind on the lee.
A Rocket was launched and the crew leapt in,
Strove with a paddle to drive east, ahead;

The skipper behind trying to join him,
But the sea bore them back, their motion dead.
Another launch made by the men, waist-deep,
She breasted a wave, they rode in the trough

And hauled up the main with the jib to keep
Sailing, thrust down the plate – lo! they were off!

Close-hauled and riding the crests, it was grand ...
'Gainst wind and tide they had sailed from the land.

SAILING OFF A LEE SHORE – 2

I was in a Foreland hauling on a line,
Inching through a tier of boats to the harbour
Steps, a stiff, north-east wind making hard labour
Of attempts to get off the beach, causing fine

Havoc as yachts were spilled on the shore. Calm
Water by the harbour wall, I gripped the rail
And held on while the yacht pitched. Bill raised the sail
As I steadied the ship with an aching arm.

Up went the genoa, up went the main, all
Hell breaking loose when the wind hit our big spread,
And coming aft Bill took the helm, turned his head,

"Right, let her go!" In with the sails and let fall
The plate ... we were at sea, riding up and down
Like jockeys at jumps, on a reach and wind blown.

SAND DUNES

Summer days have gone and cool, autumn shades
Are glowing on the beach. From south to north

It runs in a smooth, wind-swept band that fades
Not in October light as we go forth

Along its margins of grey cliff and sea,
Walking on cold sand under a deep sky.

A line of ships moored for the estuary
Await the pilot's coming to steer by
Banks and moving shoals ahead. Other tides
Have heaped the dunes that rest against the cliff,

Dunes topping green with marram grass that hides
The surface from the wind and gives belief

That new land with thistle and dock will stay ...
In other parts the old cliffs fall away.

SCAFFOLDING

Intricate as a cat's-cradle these vast
Interlacings of steel poles hug the front
Of buildings and hold them as though on last
Legs. Upright rods and cross-bars take the brunt
Of workmen's weight when they climb to the top-
Most tier with tools girdled about their hips
And scaffold boards to lay and stand on, stop-
Bars to prevent a fall and bolted clips
To lock things in place. Strong, hard, gaunt and grey-
Ribbed like an iron cage, it rears on high,
Skeleton of steel standing for a day,
Fleshless and bare, uncovered to the sky.
And when it's gone, no scars of where it's been,
Its monument a building washed and clean.

SEA

It is the natural wonder of the world,
A liquid granary replete with salt;
It rages at the shore when Neptune hurls
His trident at the heaven's stormy vault.

This magic deep, this mantle-covered power,
This universal force of azure blue,
Embraces all the Earth, creates a bower

And radiates a light, celestial blue.
Great treasury of wealth, fish-silvered store,
Caresser of the coastline, it will be

The reservoir of rivers ever more
And Evolution's heart eternally.
This crested font which blesses nascent Man
Has nurtured him since Adam's life began.

SEARCH FOR BEAUTY

I often look at faces in the street,
To scan the visage of the passer-by,
Seeking the human but elusive, sweet
Beauty, line and form that will satisfy

A yearning for perfection. Many men
Lack the grace, the refinement I prefer;
Their features ugly, bland, flat, plain, but then
'One expects them to be weathered!' was the

Comment of M'lady. How women bear
Such yokel looks I cannot understand;
Certainly some ladies are passing fair ...
Their presence is a blessing in the land.

When beauty comes it is a precious thing
And we should give it homage as a King.

'SERVE LIKE A LOOSE WOMAN'
(Tennis Coaching)

In coaching we try to mint a brief turn
Of phrase which teaches students of a sport
The finer points of play they have to learn ...
A few words, apt and memorably short.

A soccer coach who taught me years ago
At a weekend course at Kingsgate began
His lecture in the early morning glow
Of breakfast, saying, 'Look for the far man!'

I had a group of ladies on the court,
Beginners all, and we were doing 'serves';
I quipped a phrase, so memorable, I thought,
To help the squad still suffering from 'nerves'.
"Relax! Serve like a *loose* woman!" I said.
Their faces froze; disdain upon my head.

SHELTER ONE

We were given an Anderson shelter
In the early part of the war: a small
House of domed, corrugated iron set

In a pit in the lawn, reputed all
But bomb-proof, lined with concrete up to ground
Level. The dome rose barely above heads

And there we were to live and sleep when raids
Were on, night or day. We made up our beds
On mattresses on the cold, hard base; rain

Flooded in so we slept indoors in fear,
Noise of ack-ack guns permitting. Dad said
We must beware of glass if bombs fell near.

We had cracked windows, cracked walls, little sleep
But survived the Blitz, sanity to keep.

SHELTER TWO

Once it was known that Andersons were wet,
A new Morrison shelter was installed,
In house, on iron posts in the back room.

When night raids began and bombs fell, appalled
The family came downstairs and scrambled
In. On hands and knees, about a table

Height, we took cover in an iron cage
With a flat, metal roof which was able,
According to experts, to keep us safe

If the house fell in. Mother laid a cloth
On top and we sat round and dined, going
Below if the raid was hot. It served both

As table, shelter, bed where we could rest –
And we played billiards on Morrison's crest!

SHELTER THREE

Later, long before the war had ended,
For a reason I did not understand,
Builders came to the house and our indoor

Morrison cage was replaced by a brand
New, white, brick-built, reinforced, square, box-like
Thing with a thick, flat, concrete roof which took

Up half the rear garden. I suppose they
Wanted their iron back. The brick thing looked
Imposing and it protected us when

Doodlebugs and V2 rockets would fall
On our precious land and we played cricket
In the garden against the shelter wall.

And when at last the war was won in May,
The builder's men took Shelter Three away.

SHIVERING

I had a bout of shivering today,
A sharp attack that shook me to the core:
Arms, legs and trunk all trembling – I would say

I've never known such chilliness before.
In shorts and shirt, fair summer dress, I thought,
The calendar said August, summer, hot ...

But coastal winds had blustered in and caught
Me unprepared – our calendar was not!
To bed for warmth and heap on blankets thick,

The shivers lasted half an hour or so ...
Compound the trouble I was awfully sick
And cursed the yogurt I had eaten though.

Shivering, sick and feeble then I slept ...
What blessing is the health that we accept!

SIXES IN THE ELMS

The lads had gone to Orpington that day
To play a match against a village team;
The pitch was flat, the setting trim and green
And cricket was the game for men to play.
A bob was flipped, they put us in to bat
And kept our openers plodding at the crease
With a bowler, slow right arm, whose grim ease
Reduced our men to dithering format
Of style and a huge scarcity of runs.
I went in at seven to 'stop the rot',
To turn the game as the batsmen had got
Themselves dismissed like novices or nuns.
Off the grim bowler I soon made a score ...
Two sixes in the elms – and twenty more!

SONNET TO FOUR WIVES

In Morocco there is polygamy
And law allows a man to take four wives.
In England we have one throughout our lives
Or we would soon be done for bigamy.

Can you imagine – five sit down for tea
Instead of two; one will do the pouring ...
Just think of all the chat, not so wearing
When conversation's left to you and me.

But wait! Four women to every man?
Where do all these lovely ladies come from?
If there's a surplus couldn't we have some
And join the rush to lift the marriage ban?

I call upon our Ministers to say
That henceforth we can live Islamic way.

SPACE–TIME CONTINUUM

No sense of time exists in outer space,
No sense of a space–time continuum;
Time is an ancient measurement to pace
And record the speed of Earth's rotation.
We spin in annual orbit round the sun
And say it takes a year to circle it;
We note the rate of motion once begun
Before Mankind evolved to notice it.

No fleeting hours are kept upon the Moon,
Orion's Belt has neither days nor weeks,
The brightness of Sirius is a boon
To the observer who measures and seeks
To project his time in a timeless void.
We must conclude that Time is anthropoid.

SUBURBAN AIR RAID
September 1940

The Germans dropped a bomb because of flack
Which made a crater in the road's grass verge.
No one was hurt, the houses well set back,
But a gas main ignited and a surge

Of flame lit the black sky broad as next day.
A raid in progress, bombers overhead,
Ack-ack guns firing and blasting away
At planes they couldn't see, just using dead

Reckoning. House doors opened, men appeared
With spades, forks, shovels and ran
To the red, flame-flaring crater and speared
The turf in haste, shoulder to shoulder, man

To man and extinguished the gas-flame light.
Dad said, "That's it, son. Get some sleep tonight."

SUICIDE BOMBER
10 September 2001

In the news today we hear of a young
Male, suicide bomber from Palestine
Who, with explosives, nuts, bolts and nails hung
On his body, mixed with crowds on a fine

Morning in Israel and blew himself up.
He killed six people, injured many more;
Took their innocent lives – their dearest cup
Runneth over with blood – and his dark gore

Stains their memory. What evil shall fuse
In the hearts of men who devise and plan
These terrible crimes? Does their God excuse
Them when they have killed their brother man?

There is no glory in this awful crime ...
Deluded they live, not martyred in time.

SUN SIGHT TEST

The nurse came to the school to test our sight,
A starched, stiff matron, strict and hard.
The sun that day was beaming rather bright
Into the med. room where she hung her card.

With card suspended from an easel board
She stood before the window to the west
And pointed with a pencil so assured

To letters large and small that were to test
The vision of the scholars in the school.
With yellow pencil pointing in her fist,

She called me in and there I stood by rule
Which she commanded, white cuffs on her wrist.
I could not see the pencil or the line –
'Myopic!' was the verdict at the time.

SUN WORSHIP

Great golden orb enthroned upon the sky,
Which circles round our heads from day to day,
Or seems to while the Earth is spinning by,
Receive our homage, praise and ecstasy.
This burning sphere which glows with radiant heat
Gives light and life to all of us on Earth;
It pours its bounty down from street to street
And smiles upon Mankind for all it's worth.
Fountain of energy, eternal light,
Which fosters us and gives us its true leaven,
Imbues its kind with warmth and pure delight
From one great source – a Solar God in Heaven.
Can we accept that Evolution's heat
Has given birth? God bless us when we meet.

SWEDISH MILK DIET

It's a pity we have to eat so much
To stay alive. Do we overdo it?
Every few hours while we're awake such
Feasting, gormandising and we rue it
On overfill. Is it necessary
For molecule to consume molecule
While we have sunlight and water and air
To sustain us? We must not ridicule

What we need for life, but a few slices
Of bread will climb mountains and the Swedish
Milk Diet permits food which suffices
Every other day. Those who can relish

This regime will find themselves get slimmer,
Their life enduring, their paunches trimmer.

SWIMMING UNDER WATER

We were swimming at the baths, Roy and I,
Trying to hold our breath under water:

Half a width, three-quarters, another try
From one edge of the pool to the other.
Strange below the surface, no tedium
Down in the depths, kick and pull hard ahead,

Learning to live in a new medium,
Eyes open, breath held in a fluid bed.

And soon we did the length, some twenty-five
Metres from the deep end to the shallow,
Swimming below the rest after a dive,
Hoping not to hit a girl or fellow.

And sure enough, with effort, it was done ...
One breath was all we needed – it was fun.

SYMMETRY

I cannot work with papers in a heap,
With books and pencils scattered on the bench;
Things must be tidy, have a place to keep
And be there orderly or eyes will wrench
Away and want to amend a bad line.
Cushions on a seat, pictures on the wall,
Must be set and hang full-square, not decline
Or I shall notice them. On table all
Must be neatly laid to make a pattern
For the mind: knives, napkins, glasses and plates
Correctly placed or it seems a slattern
Has come to dine and that the head man hates.
What is this inner longing of the brain
That loves to see a pattern clear and plain?

TEA AT THE SAVOY

We had been to the National Gallery
In Trafalgar Square to look at the art
Of Goya, Murillo and Velázquez.

After lunch, strolling, we agreed to part
For an hour, my wife, her cousin Joan
And I, they to shop in the Strand, a schism,

While I hurried on to Fleet Street alone
To explore the realm of journalism.
A warm day in the streets brought on a thirst;

I stopped at Bert's Bar for a mug of tea;
The two ladies in The Savoy, their first
Venture, had tea in the Blue Lounge, fancy
Cakes with cream, chicken sandwiches, full rounds,
And the hotel bill came to eighteen pounds!

TEACHING TED TO SWIM

Ted could not swim; at the age of twenty-
Six he could not swim. I assured my friend,

If he fell off the Queen Elizabeth
In mid Atlantic, it would be the end.

I said I would teach him, give him lessons
At the baths. First, doggy-paddle, leg kicks
And practise putting the head in water

Until he felt comfortable; but my tricks
Did not seem to work properly with Ted.
He sank; he seemed brain-heavy; like a bear

Below the surface he held breath and swam
Breaststroke nicely until he needed air.

That's the best he can do. I'd be frantic
If I fell off ships in mid Atlantic.

THANINGTON WITHOUT

Only an English village would be called
Thanington Without; its name caught my eye
As we were in the car and driving by,
And I remarked, "It is beyond the walls

Of Canterbury, so historically
It makes some sense." But humour resisted,
"Thanington Without what?" I insisted
And felt sad that they were missing jolly

Things like running water and coffee shops,
Mullioned windows and four-poster beds,
Or even a thatched roof over their heads,
Sugar and spice and maybe organ stops.

Oh, Thanington Without, your glorious name
Will ring like Canterbury Bells in fame.

THE AGE OF WOOD

The Stone Age, Bronze Age, the Age of Iron
   Are taught to children in their history
   Lessons at school, but not the mystery
   Of the Wood Age which existed prior

To Stone. Once Man became a carnivore
And began to hunt game, then he needed
   Weapons for the kill and he succeeded
At first with clubs and wooden spears before

His animal brain turned to thoughts of stone
Shards as lethal tips for the chase. How long
It was, the Age of Wood, is not known; wrong
Thinking and no remains on the great Shore

   Of Time have left a gap that we must fill;
   The Age of Wood is bottom of the hill.

THE ARISTOCRAT

An aristocrat wrote the Shakespeare plays,
One educated and schooled at the court
Of Elizabeth Tudor. The Queen's rays
At first outshone the prodigy but taught
By Arthur Golding in Lord Burleigh's home,
The youth, ward of court to Cecil and peer
In his own right, was to rise and become
Principal star of the age; though some here
Were to allege that a raw, upstart crow
From the provinces who went to Grammar
School the while, came to town and seemed to know
Everything. Did this wife-leaver hammer
Nails in horses' hooves to get his knowledge?
'Tis certain he did not go to college.

THE ART OF POETRY

These words can never say what has passed by:
I saw a crest of gold, of beauty, peer,
Supreme. There was a quick and inward sear
Of brilliant joy when the thrill of flesh, my
Heart and mind uniting in a body
Of transmuted oneness, became a spear
Of perfect life. The lucent image clear
Faded, went; I was lost in memory,
Silently low. Pretence is my deft art;
Poets stoop to grip the elusive sand,
Kneel, etch in blood the murmurs of their heart,
Furrow for words to set down the dead brand
Of life, knowing there are those that depart
Who journeyed by and did not understand.

THE BAHAI FAITH

Baha'u'llah, the Prophet of Iran,
Seeks for all the goal of universal
Harmony: all races and creeds must ban
Discord, set apart their controversial
Differences and dwell in worldwide peace.

There is but one God therefore all must love
Him as members of one family, ease
Prejudice away and gladly approve
The equality of women and men.

The Bahai Faith teaches that all religion
Must agree with science and with reason
Or it will be seen as superstition.
If religion causes hatred and gall,
It would be better to have none at all.

THE BALL MACHINE

Three ladies at the net, each in her turn
Facing the ball machine on the base line
Shooting missiles at her. She has to spurn
The danger, face the enemy and lean
Into the shot to play a stop volley.
The ball machine, a Lobster, lowly set,
Fires a tennis ball at her every
Three seconds and she has to keep her wit

Sharp and eyes very keen. She has to smile,
Be relaxed, confident and play her shots
With conviction. Concentration the while
Wards off danger and from the coach comes lots

Of encouragement, praise galore and charm
To see his protégées don't come to harm.

THE BRIDGE TEACHER

I once bought a book on bridge, how to play,
And after a few chapters thought I would
Teach the family, show them this top game

Of cards. My wife soon proved to be a good
Player, Helen was nine, Simon, a boy
Of six, and both took to bridge like dear ducks

To water. Years went by and I lost joy
Of contract bridge, but my two lovely chicks
And my wife all continued to improve:

Mother earned county points, Helen ran clubs
At work, Simon, champion at school, loves
The game, but I retired from the rubs

Of bridge and attended a tennis course;
If I tried hard, least I could not do worse.

THE BULLDOZER, THE CRAB AND THE SEA

The sea had beached the crab upon the sand,
Half buried, dry and resting on its side:
I picked it up and took it down the strand

And laid it in a pool left by the tide.
I hoped the little fellow was not dead
And watched him drifting in a still sea-pond,

A haven for a crab to clear his head,
To wake from sleep or dreaming of beyond.
A squat machine was working in the bay

To bank the sand into a dyke or dune;
A high, spring tide expected any day
Would flood the beach with ocean very soon.
How many creatures would the waters bring
To meet their fate when tides are at the spring?

THE BUS AND THE BRIDGE

A single-decker bus came down the hill,
Passed under the bridge and went on its way.
The route of the double-decker each day
Terminated at the bridge; passengers

For the station took the up-train to town.
Bus routes and rotas had been so for years
But a new man, keen to improve, who feared
Stagnation, altered the drivers' rota,

Not knowing that habit dies hard. Big bus
Roars down the hill, new driver at the wheel,
Takes the bridge in its stride and at once feels
Resistance. Clean as could be the red top

Is sliced off like the peeling of a bow ...
Upper deck empty ... everyone below.

THE CENSUS
(April 2001)

We must complete a Census Form, confess
To Big Brother where we live, who we are,
State nationality, our faith profess,
And do we own a house or drive a car?

Why does he wish to know what I believe?
My faith, beliefs, are simply my concern:
Sceptic one day, Bahai, as I conceive,
Buddhist or Church of England as I turn.

Big Brother wants to know so many things
Which helps, he says, to govern with due care;
We also need our privacy, for Kings
Have trampled on their subjects, taxed them bare.

Big Brother must be human and benign
If we're to keep our heads, both yours and mine.

THE CHALLENGE

Two upstarts, new, young, brash, had joined the club
For badminton. They cast their eye with scorn
On old members and clearly thought them sub-
Standard. They laughed at the year they were born.
My brother, tall, fit, mature, and Old Bill,
His friend, had played the game for twenty years.
They had seen them come and go, had their fill
Of jumped-up youth who smoked and drank large beers
To prove their manhood. Then the challenge came:
They looked at Roy and Bill sitting at ease
And said, "Let's give these two old boys a game!"
Thinking that older men would break their knees
In long rallies. The game proceeded ill
For upstarts: the score? Fifteen points to nil!

THE CONSTITUTIONAL MONARCHY ASSOCIATION

If we make a case for the CMA

It is this: that we have a Head of State

Elizabeth 2nd, Her Majesty

The Queen, the living symbol of a great

Nation whose long and unique history

Extends for a thousand years, whose freedom

Is assured, envied abroad where many

Peoples are suppressed. The Queen, her kingdom,

Is above republican presidents

Who come and go with the popular vote,

Who seem to enrich themselves and are bent

By lust for power. Our dear Queen devotes

Her life to the service of the nation;

For this she deserves true admiration.

THE HARBOUR

A niche, a nook or a tiny corner
Of cold, salt sea half enclosed by an arm
Jutting from the land forms a small harbour.
The jetty curves in an embrace of calm

Water when the wind is hushed and at peace.
This haven since King Henry encloses
A handful of small boats which ply the seas
For lobster or local catches and choose

This pocket of rest as their safe demesne.
The jetty stands like a wall, hard and strong,
Against the north-east wind which tears the green
Sea to shreds when gales come gusting along.

Then the lobster boats on their moorings ride
When rough waves come knock-knocking at their side.

THE HORROR OF THE WORLD
11 September 2001

This day, God bless the passengers and crew,
Two aircraft hijacked in the US flew
Into the World Trade Centre in New York.

In a maelstrom of flame, the towers, talk
Of the globe, fell in a cloud of grey dust,
Smoke and pain. Thousands died. Watching, we just

Cry in shame. That these heartless, Godless men,
Terrorists from the East, could hope to gain
By an act so evil is delusion.

Their masters be told they preach confusion ...
Martyrdom? No. There is no paradise
For them to be; they must open their eyes

To the beauty of the natural world ...
To nothing have these terrorists been hurled.

THE INVISIBLE FIRE
(Foot and Mouth Disease, AD 2001)

The farmer waits. Distraught, he wrings his hand;
Prize herds of cattle, flocks of healthy sheep
Born in nearby farms have been killed to keep
The infection at bay, but his dear land
Is threatened by disease – all movement banned,
Footpaths closed: these dread measures make him weep,
His future in doubt. Will the virus leap
The boundaries, cross the safety zone fanned
By the west wind like invisible fire
Which scorches its victim then passes on
To tinder-dry defences. Cannot some
God stop the slaughter and its burning pyre
Of destruction? Once these fine herds have gone
England will be barren for ages come.

THE METRIC MARTYR

Will the length of King Edward's arm be next?
Our measures, weights, the pint, our native mile?
And all because a European text
Takes precedence o'er English law the while.

A grocer sells bananas by the pound,
They should be metric under Brussels' law;
But people in these lands have always found
Imperial ways much better; they abhor

The rule of European courts abroad,
Prefer to keep their heritage their own,
Retain pound sterling, hold their great accord,
All kingdoms past, the virtue they have shown.

O let us keep this island's sovereignty
And thank God for the comfort of the sea!

THE PHILOSPHER AND THE CHEESE-MITE'S LEG

I am impatient with philosophy,
Speculation on Nature and Being,
The cheese-mite's leg, a steeple's height, for we
Can do better than that, B. R. Seeing
Is believing, they say. I have never
Seen a cheese-mite or measured a steeple.
Ours doesn't vary – it's been there ever
And a day. The book was a bore. People
I know prefer earthly things, sound and sense,
Not abstracts and fifty pages of proof.
As impatient man give me pounds and pence,
Trees, houses, hills and you may stand aloof.
For all his metaphysics his dinner
Wasn't abstract or he'd have been thinner!

THE PRESIDENT OF IRAN

Allah praise the President of Iran,
Mr Khatami, modern, moderate;
With the support of youth he is the man
To bring the nation to the golden gate

Or reform. In recent times the old guard
Of conservative, Islamic mullahs
Have checked the yearning for freedom, have barred
The wishes of the young for a fuller

Pro-Western role in mores and in dress,
Have jailed intellectuals and students
For protest and have closed parts of the press.
Girls still cover their heads like nuns but vent

Their feelings for change whenever they may;
Thousands leave Iran for a better way.

THERE ARE NO CLOCKS AND WATCHES

There are no clocks and watches in the sky,
No sundials, calendars, thermometers
In space. There, time has no chronometers
To register its beat, though endlessly
It pulses here each day upon this Earth.
Aware of daily events afforded
By the sun, we zealously recorded
Each grey dawn and pink sunset for their worth

And projected our notion of Earth's time
Into the deeps of space where stars and gas
Clouds form galaxies of gigantic mass
Without time's sense of reason or of rhyme.
The only place where time is said to be
Is here on Earth – and here it's time for tea!

THE RED ARROWS

Above the sea in August, summer sky
The nine of diamonds, bright, royal flush,
Were aerial and flying, aces high,
This happy day. A many thousand crush,

All eagerly awaiting when they came,
Nine as but one in perfect line of flight,
Purest red and white, Harriers by name,
And banked above the coast, a thrilling sight.

Swan Loop and Goose the Caterpillar mode,
Big Vixen Roll and Vixen Break – to show
Their skill the pilots uttered jets of smoke
To trace the sky: red, white and blue ... and so
Our tribute to the Arrows is unfurled –
They are the peak, the Fliers of the World.

THE ROCK POOL

Shallow it lay, clear as a crystal ball
On the sand-set shore, warm-watered and still,
Reflecting the sky above with clouds all
Feathered and white, delicate as a rill
In a meadow. Beyond the pool the beach
Ran northly to chalk cliffs at the headland,
South to a pocket harbour, both in reach
Of a short walk. In the rock pool clear sand

Lay six inches down and two little girls
Had this warm pond to themselves, where they dipped
And scooped the liquid grains of gold in swirls
Of placid contentment. Dear Helen tripped

By, watching her little ones at their play;
The beach was hers all morning of that day.

THE SHORE OF TIME

I sit on sands of ageless time gone by,
While last year's tide is lacing on the shore;
Tomorrow's sun, attendant in the sky,
Is casting off its light as though before.
And children here, born on this step of time,
Bemused by sand and sea and playful air
Are held in roseate wonder, love and rhyme
And see not half the beauty that is here.
Beneath the void and touching, changeless sea,
Lapped by its channel waters blue and warm,
Earth's mothers sit in vigil happily,
Love's monument of their eternal charm.
I could but think in this dear evening's glow
It's now, and was, a thousand years ago.

THE SONG THRUSH

Awaking at the coming of the day
And peering from the haven of his bush,
He feathers down to make his first essay
Of snails; my friend, the singing-anvil thrush.
His breast a tawny cream or tawny mouse,
A chequerboard of colour in his name,
He lingers near the window of my house
And reads the menu posted on the frame.
He loiters while he makes his choice of food:
A slithey worm, some snail's delicious dish,
And says the cuisine is the best – how good
Of him in song to compliment and wish
For more! I watch him, save the aftermath,
Where he is whopping snails upon the path.

THE SOUL OF MAN

Let us now analyse the human soul:
By definition it is said to be
Mind, spirit, embodied, disembodied,
That part of Man which thinks, feels, desires,
But isn't this an attribute of Mind?

Mind thinks; it is the seat of our feelings ...
Mind is the crucible of our desires ...
Mind is a function of the human brain ...
Mind, soul and spirit we cannot equate ...

Two are but vague cousins of the other,
So of three the Mind is acceptable,
That quality of brain set in the skull
Which is its proper home. There it resides,
The better part of Man while he's alive.

THE STEPS OF PARADISE

Twilight, so still, beneath a sky of blue,
Teased with serried cloud, purest pale and white,
A windless eve, so calm, and rich in hue,
And swifts come flying, sixty in my sight.
They dip and rise above the June-leaf trees,
In flight as true as Eros' guided darts;
They veer, circle in silence, black as bees
In dimmer light when twilight fades and parts.
The stillness marked a presence in my mind
As though the God Aeolus held his breath
And breathed nor or caused any wisp of wind
To break a peace that had long endureth.
Oh, this is solemn pleasure in my eyes,
A feast upon the steps of Paradise.

THE TRUE SHAKESPEARE

17th Earl of Oxford, Edward de Vere,
Is the true Shakespeare, author of the plays
Said to have been written by Will, a mere
Countrified lad from Stratford, whose wild ways
And early marriage to Anne equipped him,
It is believed, for the task of writing
Verse, sonnets and great drama at the whim
Of genius. Nothing uninviting
About this – Oh, no! It's all in accord
With mere genius, of course; no schooling
Required, no books, background; he'd be bored
If he had to learn something while fooling
About with deer. Can we not now assume
That Will Shakespeare was Oxford's nom de plume?

THE WINDS ARE KEEN

At evening as the vernal sun is setting,
I sit and watch the fading light go down,
And love the April heat that we are getting
Instead of rain in which the gardens drown.
This sunlight swelling through the pane blesses
Those of us who need shelter from the wind
Which tears in from the sea, ruffling dresses
And coats awry – Oh, this is most unkind!
We coastal folk who live by England's shore
Are blown apart from east and west and north.
We tolerate the blast, no wish for more,
And long for calmer days when we go forth.
The winds are keen which scythe in off the sea –
We'll have it warm when summer paints the lea.

THIS EARTHLY PARADISE

Do men not know this Earthly Paradise?
It was so in Eden. Adam and Eve
Were dispossessed but we have realised,
Inherited God's gift and now conceive
The garden to be bigger than first thought.
It extends throughout the Earth, produces
Corn, rice, fish, fruit as we have all been taught
But forget to wonder. Priest induces
Us to believe his Heaven; it's explained
To the immortal-minded – this is wrong.
Paradise lost is paradise regained
If we but think it so. It is a song
We should glory in, expectant brother;
Paradise is *here* – there is no other!

TONY'S LIFE

We moored the yacht a quarter after three ...
An inlet that was running by the stream,
Resolving we would make a brew of tea
And rest awhile; the wind had blown abeam
Blustery all day. Tony went on deck

To clear the pot but failed to return soon
As he should. Quite alarmed I craned my neck
Out – he had gone overboard! Cups and spoons
Abandoned I ran for'ard – no splash, sound,
Ripple nor cry; at the bow finger-tips

On the coaming. "Bob!" Quickly looking round,
Saw an arm above the surface; he'd tripped,
Fallen in feet first – and he couldn't swim!
I grabbed a wrist, hauled, helped to rescue him.

TWO CANNIBALS

How clever the men who produce good jokes!
    Not the comedians who make us laugh,
    Like Tommy Cooper, the funniest bloke
    Ever, but script-writers, joke-makers half

    A league ahead of the rest of us, who
Have very sharp wits and humour in the mind.
    Surely all of us love stories and do
    Admire their skill. It would not be unkind

    To write a joke: two cannibals were ship-
    Wrecked on a desert isle with no water,
    No food for three weeks, not even a blip
    On the skyline ... all was lost! No matter,

    They lit a fire, each smiled at his brother ...
    Both were so hungry ... they ate each other!

UGLY BEASTS

What ugly beasts have roamed the planet Earth!

Grotesque and massive, monstrous to behold,
A product of Creation they gave birth

To monsters in the ages to unfold.
We cannot now believe they were our kin,
A branch of evolution gone astray?

And yet they were the tenants well within
The regions we've inherited today.
And were these monsters part of God's command,
To populate the Earth with creatures rude?

Or did the scheme get somewhat out of hand
Before a modern race became imbued
With grace and beauty of the human kind,
With creatures that the Laws of Life refined?

UNCLE HARRY

Uncle Harry, a small man with a marine
Nose, a thirst for beer and smoking his own
Cigarettes which he rolled in a machine
Very slowly, fumbling with his short, brown
Fingers while, eyes upon the roller, he
Talked to us at home. Welcome visitor
He was because he could talk endlessly
Without breath it seemed. An inquisitor

After knowledge he impressed with great yarns
Of fishing at Cookham, drinking in pubs,
As though the be all of this life was barns
Of brown ale to be consumed in pots, tubs

And glasses. How that man could talk and drink!
His tongue awash, it helped him smoke and think.

UNCLE HARRY AND THE DE LUXE MODEL SHED

A long time ago before DIY
Was known, Uncle Harry purchased a shed.
When the parts were delivered his red eye

Popped – a thousand pieces made his poor head
Ache: sides, struts, front, back, a door and a roof
Of asbestos sheets, pipes and two gutters

With brackets to keep it dry and proof
Against the rain. Harry, in a flutter,
Had bolts, nuts and screws and a very long

List of instructions: How To Assemble
A De Luxe Shed – but bits didn't belong,
He found, far too many to resemble

The model he had in mind: hence the frown
When he built the De Luxe roof upside down!

UNCLE TOM

Uncle Tom, on my father's side, was tall,
Quiet, sleepy, shrewd, reclusive, able
To live on one night's work a week. That's all;
One night, Saturday, on a notable

London newspaper. On the other six
Days he rested at home and studied form:
The horses, racing, gee-gees, and he'd fix
Bets with his bookmaker, tune in and warm

To the radio for news of winners.
Tom would wager a quid on the second
Favourite; good odds would pay his dinners;
Pound patent, union jack were reckoned

To keep him in sterling and see him fed ...
That shrewd, old dreamer was fond of his bed.

VOICES

I love to hear the sound of a good voice

In speech, in song; I love its melody,
Its timbre, accent, warmth, its charm and my choice

Is that of quality, not threnody
At death or unaccompanied singing,
But the clear, cultivated voice of man

Or woman whose fine tone is entrancing:
Churchill, Roosevelt, Peter Finch ... I'd ban

Many public figures; they cannot speak;
No voice, poor diction; they have no idea
How bad they are; they should listen each week

To Greer Garson, Deborah Kerr, have ear
To lovely sound, its melody above.

Sian Lloyd's a voice I like and do approve.

VOICES OF SUMMER

Now the beach is empty, the children gone,
And the salt winds blow on the barren sand ...
The glad voices of summer linger on
Below the high cliffs where the beach-huts stand
In isolation. The lonely sea sounds

The shore and seagulls cry in winged flight,
Gliding on the crest's uplift, wheeling round

The silence below where they played so light
Of heart, idyllic in the sun. Will they

Come again when winter and desolate
Seas have crossed these shores and washed the bare bay
With chilling tides? They will return to prate,
Shout and play in the shallows of the sea ...
A joy to watch our children's ecstasy.

VULGARITY IS NECESSARY
Report in the Times, 11 April 2001

From *The Times* we do expect better things,

Not their defence of coarseness and bad taste;

Yet their writer insists the life of Kings

Is fodder to the mass that should not waste.

He said that gossip, slander, even sleaze

Is called for – it will make the paper sell,

And where truth is lacking, if it will please

The simple reader – truth is stretched as well.

News hounds harry folk, intrude and report

On privacy in print and photograph,

And seem to regard the practice as sport

That is lawful among the paper's staff.

To cap it all he wrote this heresy:

That vulgarity is necessary!

WALKING

One foot in front of the other, one breath
To feed it and we are haply moving:

Upright, body and soul on its limbs, death
Far away, we float on pure air, loving
The earth beneath us and feeling as strong.

Out in the hills upon the furry grass,
Treading a highway or hiking along
Field tracks and bridle-paths our pleasures pass
With us, blood alert, air upon the cheek,

Eye resting upon a fine, green feature;
And feeling so, we could walk for a week,
For ever, such is a human creature.

Though we stride upon earth for one short span,
It is the finest attribute of Man.

WASPS

They're busy in the roof space overhead:
Wasps, insidious creatures, nasty pests,
Are toiling in the dark to build their nest
Two feet above me in the study. Dread
Does not concern me but they spoiled my work,
So I began a campaign to disturb
Their circadian rhythms; could I curb
Their industry, move them on, I would perk

Up ... tried tapping the white, alcove ceiling
With a ruler, a steady beat, a tune,
Syncopation, jazz, thinking it would soon
Stop their intrusion. They hurt my feelings

By boring through a polystyrene tile –
I called Pest Control – made them run a mile!

WESTERNS

I love western films and cowboys with guns,
Their shirts, scarves and Stetsons, their John Wayne slacks,
The horses they ride, the bays, whites and duns,

Dust clouds raised up when they gallop on tracks;
The saloons, wooden sidewalks and stables,
Bales of hay, rough roof-beams and lowly troughs

Of water, lanterns, banks, poker tables
Where stern-faced 'pokes look worried when Doc coughs;
The long bars where the thirsty drovers stand

And call for 'Whisky!' to clear dry, trail dust
From stubbled throats, and gunplay on a hand
Of marked cards when the loser's flush is bust;

Yul Brynner, Steve McQueen, all the seven
In a film, a classic western – Heaven!

WHAT TO TEACH A CHILD

First teach a child to speak and then to read,
Give him books for knowledge and for pleasure,
Give him all your love, measure by measure,

Let him run, climb, swim and play – he will need
Strength of body, mind and heart – and then teach
Obedience, honesty, discipline,

Respect for others, life and God, and sing
To instil love of song, music, that each
May have beauty in his heart. Let him make

Things, build, paint, plant a garden and create
Flowers, food. And, dear father and mother,
You should provide a sister or brother.

In all, if you would make him like a King,
Then do your best to teach him everything!

WHEN HELEN COMES

When Helen comes she brings a waft of air,
A daughter dear reminding me of when,
In fresher years, she grew to be so fair
And lovely as a child, so loving then
And now. She brings two children of her own,
Two daughters made as pretty as the dew –

Dappled rose, new budded, still yet part grown
But destined for their mother's beauty too.

A daughter and her darlings ranging here,
Eloquent and charming when she complies
As artist, teacher, actress full of cheer,
An ever-loving comfort if one cries.

This child of mine, full-eyed when she was born,
Shines with the strength of sunlight in the dawn.

WHY CAN'T WE EAT GRASS?

Why can't we eat grass? Doesn't it seem strange
That Man has evolved on this Earth over
Countless aeons of time, treading the range
Of grasslands, steppes, prairies, its green cover,
Without being able to eat the stuff?

Cows eat grass, bulls, deer, sheep, and elephants
Feed on foliage – they're all strong enough,
But Man has to labour over crop plants
And harvest them for food: lettuce, kale, chives,
Store them, wash them, cook them for his dinner,

Rear beef, lamb, venison, pork all his life ...
Why can't he eat grass? Would men be thinner,
Fat as bulls or mellow as dumb, brown cows,
Placid, cud-chewing, free from warlike rows?

WHY DO CARS OVERTAKE?

Like so many of my unblemished peers

I am obliged to state and to record
That I have been driving some forty years

Without killing any person on board,
Or on the main road, not even a cat.
I poodle along at a modest speed

Without exceeding the limit and that
Is an achievement, I'm told. Do take heed
Racing drivers, who invariably

Sit on my tail, swerve out and roar ahead!

Why do they hurry so impatiently
While I look at daffodils in their bed?
If I were a Minister on the make,
I would reward those who don't overtake!

WOMEN WHO CAN TALK

How is it that women can talk so well?
I can hear Martina N. chattering

On TV, her monotone like a bell
Of small, musical range. Not flattering?

No, she does not pause for breath but chats right
On. This inherited ability

In speech began in the cave; the men fight
For breath while chasing game, facility

They need or no one eats, and when they come
Home, hurt, dirty, exhausted by the chase,

They are too worn to tell the women some
Of their concerns that day; they rest and face

Their children's laughter with the briefest word
And listen to the talkers from the herd.

WORD PROCESSOR

I had to buy a new word-processor
To replace the one I had used almost
Daily for over six years. Possessor

Of a Canon Starwriter Five Thousand,
I lament still the demise of the old
Machine: the bubble-jet cartridge failing

To print, refusing to run in its bold
Track along its steel bar, dust, grit, fluff, gunge
Clogging the moving parts. Strange! It never

Occurred to me to have the thing serviced;
I assumed it would go on for ever!
And then the shock – my beloved machine

Seized up, expired, its inner parts quite *morte*.
But now I smile – my new one is well bought.

WORTHY OF HIS HIRE

He plunged his arm in an Icelandic sea;
A sprain or tendon damage in the wrist.
Cold compress is the treatment, therapy
He said, and soaked the limb. There'd been a twist
Of white cotton for support, but he had
Duties in the garden with hoe and spade,
Young lettuce, spinach, onions, and a bad
Arm rendered him half useless at his trade.
The labourer in the vineyard could earn
A penny for the day and he would need
Two arms for the harvest, trimming of the stern
Vine – let the one-armed man recite the creed:
In the heat of day when lesser men perspire
The labourer is worthy of his hire.